The False Promise:

The Myth of Democracy, Globalist Agendas, and the Case for Anarcho-Capitalism

Mark Winters

The False Promise: The Myth of Democracy, Globalist Agendas, and the Case for Anarcho-Capitalism

Author Mark Winters

Published By Neil McKenzie

ISBN 9781326927158
Imprint: Lulu.com

Chapter 1:

Introduction :

The Illusion of Democracy

The Egyptian Revolution and the False Promise of Democracy

In early 2011, millions of Egyptians took to the streets, demanding the resignation of their long-time authoritarian ruler, Hosni Mubarak. What began as a series of small protests quickly evolved into a nationwide revolution, fuelled by a shared belief that democracy would bring freedom, equality, and justice to a nation long oppressed by tyranny. After 18 days of relentless protest, Mubarak stepped down, and the Egyptian people celebrated what they believed was the dawn of a new democratic era.

Yet, within two years, the dream of democracy turned into a nightmare. Mohamed Morsi, the country's first democratically elected president, was overthrown in a military coup, and the nation descended into political chaos once again. The revolution that had promised so much brought little change. Egypt's experiment with democracy did not deliver on its promise to the people; instead, it cemented the power of military elites, plunged the country into deeper turmoil, and left many questioning whether democracy was truly the solution to their problems.

This example is emblematic of a broader reality: democracy, as it is often practiced today, is not the great liberating force it is portrayed to be. Instead of being a system that serves the people, democracy has increasingly become a tool for control—manipulated by elites to maintain power, subdue dissent, and impose their agendas on the masses. Far from fulfilling the ideals of freedom and self-governance, modern democracy often operates as a veneer for the very systems of oppression it claims to oppose.

What is Democracy? The Ideal vs. The Reality

At its core, democracy is defined as a system of government in which power is vested in the people, either directly or through elected representatives. The idea is that through free and fair elections, citizens can choose leaders who reflect their interests and hold them accountable through regular voting cycles. In theory, democracy ensures that government authority is derived from the will of the majority, while protecting the rights of minorities. It promises individual freedoms, equality before the law, and a political system that reflects the diverse values and interests of the population.

However, the democracy of textbooks and political speeches bears little resemblance to the democracy that exists in most nations today. In practice, modern democracies are often plagued by crony capitalism, elite manipulation, and systemic corruption. Instead of empowering individuals, they concentrate power in the hands of a political and corporate elite. Instead of facilitating genuine political choice, they offer carefully curated options that reflect the interests of powerful global actors rather than the will of the people.

Elections in modern democracies are frequently influenced by corporate donations, media manipulation, and lobbying by powerful interest groups. Political campaigns often become competitions between wealthy elites, who use their financial resources to dominate the public discourse and drown out alternative voices. Meanwhile, key decisions affecting the lives of millions are increasingly made by unelected bureaucrats, global institutions, and multinational corporations, far removed from the scrutiny of the people they claim to serve.

Central Thesis: Democracy as a Tool for Control

The central argument of this chapter—and indeed, the book as a whole—is that democracy, far from being a system of government that empowers individuals, has become a tool for control. It is used by elites and globalists to maintain their grip on power, suppress dissent, and impose policies that serve their interests, often at the expense of the broader population.

At its core, democracy as practiced today is not about giving people a voice. It is about creating the illusion of choice, while ensuring that the real decisions are made by a small group of political, corporate, and financial elites. By holding periodic elections and allowing limited political competition, modern democracies pacify the masses and create the appearance of legitimacy. But the choices offered in elections are often shallow, and the outcomes are heavily influenced by powerful interests behind the scenes.

In this way, democracy functions as a form of controlled opposition. It allows people to believe they have a say in how they are governed, while in reality, the key levers of power remain in the hands of the same elites, regardless of which political party or leader is elected. This creates a system where fundamental change is nearly impossible, and the status quo is maintained, no matter how dissatisfied the population may be.

The Role of Globalism in Undermining Democracy

One of the primary forces undermining democracy today is globalism—the idea that political and economic power should be centralised in international institutions and controlled by a global elite. While globalism is often portrayed as a force for cooperation and peace, in reality, it serves the interests of multinational corporations, international financial institutions, and supranational organisations like the United Nations, the World Economic Forum (WEF), and the International Monetary Fund (IMF).

Globalism seeks to erode national sovereignty and local control, replacing it with a global governance structure that is less accountable to the people and more responsive to the needs of the elite. This globalist agenda is often advanced through trade agreements, international treaties, and regulations that supersede national laws and limit the ability of citizens to influence policy. For example, trade agreements like the Trans-Pacific Partnership (TPP) and the North American Free Trade Agreement (NAFTA) have often been negotiated in secret, with little input from ordinary citizens, yet they have profound effects on national economies, labour markets, and individual rights.

Through these mechanisms, globalists are able to impose policies that favour large corporations and financial institutions, while undermining the sovereignty of nation-states and the autonomy of individuals. This centralisation of power is fundamentally at odds with the democratic ideal, which is based on the idea of local control and self-governance. As more decisions are made at the global level, the ability of citizens to influence their own governments diminishes, and democracy becomes little more than a façade.

Crony Capitalism: The Economic Arm of Control

Democracy's illusion of freedom is also undermined by the rise of crony capitalism—a system in which businesses and governments collude to create monopolies, manipulate markets, and suppress competition. Under crony capitalism, powerful corporations use their wealth and influence to secure government favours, such as subsidies, bailouts, and regulatory protections, while smaller competitors are pushed out of the market. This creates a system in which economic power is concentrated in the hands of a few large corporations, which in turn use their influence to shape government policy in their favour.

Crony capitalism undermines the principles of both democracy and free-market capitalism. Instead of allowing individuals and businesses to compete on a level playing field, it distorts the market by giving unfair advantages to politically connected corporations. This not only stifles innovation and competition but also erodes public trust in the political system, as citizens see their governments catering to the interests of a wealthy elite rather than representing the will of the people.

The influence of crony capitalism can be seen in industries like finance, agriculture, and healthcare, where large corporations receive preferential treatment from governments, while smaller businesses and consumers bear the brunt of the costs. For example, during the 2008 financial crisis, governments around the world bailed out large banks and financial institutions, while ordinary citizens lost their homes, jobs, and savings. Similarly, in the healthcare industry, pharmaceutical companies use their influence to shape government policy, securing patents and regulatory protections that allow them to charge exorbitant prices for life-saving medications.

In a truly democratic system, the government would serve as a check on corporate power, ensuring that the market remains competitive and that the interests of ordinary citizens are protected. However, in modern democracies, the lines between government and business have become increasingly blurred, and the government often acts as a partner to corporate elites rather than a defender of the people.

Anarcho-Capitalism: A Solution to the Illusion?

In contrast to the centralised control of democracy and crony capitalism, anarcho-capitalism offers a vision of a truly free society—one in which individuals are not subject to the coercive power of the state or the manipulation of globalist elites. Anarcho-capitalism is based on the principles of volunteerism, private property, and the non-aggression principle, which holds that individuals should be free to live their lives as they choose, as long as they do not initiate force or coercion against others.

In an anarcho-capitalist society, there would be no central government to impose laws or regulations. Instead, individuals would enter into voluntary contracts with one another, and disputes would be resolved through private arbitration or community-based systems of justice. Economic transactions would take place in a free market, without government intervention or corporate favouritism, and individuals would be free to create their own systems of governance, security, and infrastructure.

While this vision may seem radical, it is based on the idea that true freedom and prosperity can only be achieved in the absence of coercive power structures. By rejecting the illusions of democracy and crony capitalism, anarcho-capitalism offers a path to a society where individuals are free to pursue their own interests, create their own communities, and build a future based on voluntary cooperation and mutual benefit.

Preview of Key Arguments

Throughout the rest of this book, I will argue that the illusion of democracy serves as a mechanism of control, allowing global elites to maintain their power while pacifying the masses with the appearance of choice. I will explore how crony capitalism undermines both democracy and free-market principles, and how globalism seeks to centralise power in the hands of unelected international institutions.

In later chapters, I will delve deeper into the globalist agenda, examining the ways in which multinational corporations, international financial institutions, and supranational organisations work together to shape global policy in their Favour. I will also make the moral and practical case for anarcho-capitalism as a solution to the problems created by democracy and crony capitalism, offering a vision for a future in which individuals are truly free to govern themselves.

Ultimately, this book seeks to challenge the commonly accepted narrative that democracy is the best and only path to freedom. Instead, I will argue that true freedom can only be achieved by rejecting the illusions of democracy, crony capitalism, and globalism, and embracing a system of voluntary cooperation and individual autonomy.

Chapter 2:

Capitalism in Chains: The Globalist Hijacking

Capitalism, as an economic system, has long been synonymous with the pursuit of individual freedom, innovation, and prosperity. Rooted in the principles of free markets, voluntary exchange, and personal responsibility, capitalism was intended to empower individuals to achieve success through their efforts and entrepreneurial endeavours. However, what we witness today bears little resemblance to the pure, unfettered system of free-market capitalism envisioned by classical economists like Adam Smith.

Instead, modern capitalism has been co-opted, manipulated, and distorted by a web of alliances between powerful corporations, governments, and international organisations. This unholy alliance has given rise to what is often referred to as "crony capitalism"—a system where political influence and government power are used to secure corporate dominance, eliminate competition, and consolidate wealth in the hands of the elite.

In this chapter, we will explore how globalist agendas, driven by a desire for centralised control, have hijacked the principles of capitalism. Through historical analysis, case studies, and contemporary examples, we will expose the mechanisms of crony capitalism and how it has undermined free markets, stifled innovation, and eroded individual freedom.

The Roots of Capitalism: A System of Free Markets

To understand the globalist hijacking of capitalism, it is important to first examine its origins. Capitalism, as an economic system, emerged in the late 18th century as a response to the limitations of feudalism and mercantilism. Central to capitalism is the idea of private property, voluntary exchange, and the allocation of resources through market mechanisms rather than state control.

The foundations of capitalist thought were laid by Adam Smith in his seminal work, The Wealth of Nations (1776). Smith argued that individuals, acting in their self-interest within a competitive marketplace, would unintentionally contribute to the greater good of society. He described this phenomenon as the "invisible hand," where the pursuit of profit by individuals leads to increased efficiency, innovation, and wealth creation for all.

Smith's vision of capitalism was one where government intervention was minimal, limited to enforcing contracts, protecting property rights, and ensuring national defence. In a truly free market, businesses would rise or fall based on their ability to meet the needs of consumers, incentivising efficiency and competition. The market, not the state, would determine the allocation of resources, the distribution of wealth, and the pace of technological progress.

However, the purity of Smith's vision was short-lived. As industrialisation advanced and global trade expanded, new forces emerged that sought to subvert the principles of free markets and replace them with a system of control—control wielded by a small group of political and corporate elites.

The Rise of Crony Capitalism: From Industrialisation to Globalism

The first major distortion of capitalism began during the Industrial Revolution. As businesses grew in size and complexity, many began to seek government favours to secure their market dominance. These favours often came in the form of tariffs, subsidies, and other forms of protectionism that shielded established industries from competition.

One of the most prominent examples of early crony capitalism was the creation of monopolies through government-granted charters. In industries such as railroads, oil, and steel, large corporations colluded with politicians to secure exclusive rights to resources, transportation routes, or markets. This collusion often resulted in the suppression of smaller competitors, reduced innovation, and inflated prices for consumers.

John D. Rockefeller's Standard Oil is a classic case of crony capitalism in action. While Rockefeller's initial success was due to his innovative business practices, his company eventually used its size and influence to gain preferential treatment from the government, including favourable railroad rates that smaller competitors could not access. This allowed Standard Oil to dominate the oil industry and stifle competition. Rockefeller's monopoly was eventually broken up by the U.S. government under antitrust laws, but only after decades of market distortion.

As capitalism evolved into the 20th century, the relationship between business and government deepened. Corporations increasingly relied on political connections to secure lucrative contracts, gain regulatory advantages, and suppress new entrants into their industries. This dynamic was particularly evident in the defence sector, where companies like Lockheed Martin and Boeing benefited from government contracts and lobbying efforts that secured their dominance in military procurement.

By the time the 21st century arrived, crony capitalism had become a global phenomenon. The rise of multinational corporations, the growth of international trade, and the formation of global governance institutions like the International Monetary Fund (IMF) and World Trade Organisation (WTO) created new avenues for corporate-government collusion on an unprecedented scale. The global financial system, once a hallmark of free-market capitalism, became a tool for enriching the few at the expense of the many.

Globalist Agendas and the Hijacking of Capitalism

In the modern era, the hijacking of capitalism by globalist interests has reached new heights. The goal of globalist elites is not merely to distort markets but to centralise economic and political power on a global scale. This agenda is pursued through a variety of mechanisms, including the creation of supranational organisations, the manipulation of financial markets, and the consolidation of corporate power.

The globalist vision of capitalism is one where large corporation operate with impunity, free from the constraints of national sovereignty or democratic accountability. Under this system, governments act as enforcers of corporate interests, implementing policies that protect the profits of multinational companies while undermining the economic freedom of individuals.

One of the key mechanisms through which globalist agendas are advanced is the use of international trade agreements. While these agreements are often presented as tools for promoting free trade, they are, in reality, designed to benefit large corporations at the expense of smaller businesses and workers. Trade agreements like the North American Free Trade Agreement (NAFTA) and the Trans-Pacific Partnership (TPP) include provisions that grant corporations the power to challenge national laws and regulations that threaten their profits. These provisions, known as investor-state dispute settlement (ISDS) mechanisms, allow corporations to sue governments in international tribunals, bypassing domestic courts and undermining national sovereignty.

Another tool of globalist control is the centralisation of monetary policy through institutions like the Federal Reserve, the European Central Bank, and the Bank for International Settlements. These institutions have the power to manipulate interest rates, control the money supply, and create inflation or deflation at will. By controlling the flow of money, central banks can influence economic activity, benefiting large financial institutions while impoverishing ordinary citizens.

The global financial crisis of 2008 provides a clear example of how globalist interests manipulate capitalism for their own gain. The crisis, which was triggered by the reckless behaviour of large financial institutions, resulted in massive bailouts for banks while millions of ordinary people lost their homes and jobs. Governments around the world, under pressure from international financial institutions, implemented austerity measures that further impoverished their populations, all while ensuring that the profits of the financial elite remained intact.

Case Studies: The Globalist Hijacking in Action

1. The 2008 Financial Crisis: Bailouts for the Elite

The 2008 financial crisis is perhaps the most glaring example of how crony capitalism has taken root at the highest levels of the global financial system. The crisis was triggered by the collapse of the U.S. housing bubble, which was fuelled by reckless lending practices and the proliferation of complex financial instruments like mortgage-backed securities. As the housing market imploded, banks and financial institutions that had taken on massive amounts of risk found themselves on the verge of collapse.

In a truly free-market system, these institutions would have been allowed to fail, as they had made irresponsible decisions that led to their downfall. However, instead of letting the market correct itself, governments around the world stepped in to bail out the banks, using taxpayer money to rescue institutions that had created the crisis in the first place. In the U.S., the Troubled Asset Relief Program (TARP) provided $700 billion in bailout funds to major banks, while the Federal Reserve pumped trillions of dollars into the financial system through quantitative easing.

The result was a massive transfer of wealth from ordinary citizens to the financial elite. While millions of people lost their homes, jobs, and savings, the banks that had caused the crisis emerged stronger than ever. Not only were they bailed out, but many of the same executives responsible for the risky practices that led to the collapse received large bonuses in the aftermath of the crisis.

2. The U.S. Big Bank Bailouts: Too Big to Fail?

The 2008 financial crisis exposed the true extent of crony capitalism at the highest levels of global finance. One of the most infamous aspects of the crisis was the concept of "too big to fail," where certain financial institutions were deemed so large and integral to the global economy that their failure was considered unacceptable. This concept became the justification for massive government bailouts of some of the world's largest banks, a process that epitomised the globalist hijacking of capitalism.

Among the largest beneficiaries of these bailouts were banks such as JPMorgan Chase, Citigroup, and Bank of America. These institutions had engaged in high-risk lending and speculative trading, particularly in the housing market, which ultimately triggered the crisis. Rather than allowing these banks to fail and letting the market recalibrate, the U.S. government intervened with the Troubled Asset Relief Program (TARP), which allocated over $700 billion to bail out these failing institutions.

In a truly free-market capitalist system, businesses that make bad investments or take on excessive risk should face the consequences of their actions, including bankruptcy. However, the "too big to fail" doctrine undermined this fundamental principle by creating a system in which large corporations could take massive risks, secure in the knowledge that the government would step in to save them if things went wrong. This arrangement not only distorted the market but also created moral hazard, as it incentivised banks to continue engaging in risky behaviour, knowing they would be bailed out in the future.

The bailouts also revealed the deep connections between the financial sector and government officials, many of whom had worked for or had close ties to the very institutions they were rescuing. For example, Henry Paulson, the U.S. Treasury Secretary at the time of the crisis, was a former CEO of Goldman Sachs, one of the major beneficiaries of the government's bailout efforts. This revolving door between Wall Street and Washington epitomised the crony capitalist system, where corporate elites and government officials work hand in hand to protect their mutual interests.

While the banks were bailed out, ordinary citizens were left to bear the brunt of the crisis. Millions lost their homes, jobs, and life savings, while the financial elite emerged relatively unscathed. The inequality generated by the crisis and the subsequent bailout highlighted the fundamental injustice of crony capitalism and the globalist agendas that perpetuate it.

3. Government Subsidies: The Case of Big Agriculture

Another industry that provides a clear example of crony capitalism is agriculture. In many developed countries, including the United States and the European Union, governments provide billions of dollars in subsidies to large agribusiness corporations. These subsidies are often justified on the grounds of protecting national food security and supporting small farmers. However, in practice, the majority of these subsidies go to large, wealthy agribusinesses that already dominate the market, while small, independent farmers struggle to survive.

In the United States, for example, the top 10% of subsidy recipients receive nearly 80% of all agricultural subsidies, according to the Environmental Working

Group. These subsidies often go to large, industrial farms that produce crops like corn, soybeans, and wheat. Small farmers, on the other hand, receive little to no government support and are often forced out of business due to the competitive pressures created by the subsidised agribusiness giants.

The distortion of the agricultural market through subsidies creates numerous negative consequences. First, it stifles innovation and competition, as large agribusinesses have little incentive to improve efficiency or explore sustainable farming practices when they are guaranteed government support. Second, it leads to the overproduction of certain crops, which can depress global commodity prices and harm farmers in developing countries who do not receive similar subsidies. Third, it contributes to environmental degradation, as industrial farming practices—such as monoculture and heavy pesticide use—are often unsustainable in the long term.

These agricultural subsidies are a prime example of how government intervention in the market distorts competition and entrenches the dominance of established corporations. Rather than allowing the market to determine the most efficient and innovative farming practices, crony capitalism in the agricultural sector props up large corporations at the expense of small farmers and consumers.

4. Lobbying: Corporate Influence Over Policy

The pervasive influence of corporate lobbying in shaping government policy is another key feature of crony capitalism. In a truly free market, businesses would compete based on their ability to provide goods and services that meet the needs of consumers. However, in today's crony capitalist system, many corporations instead focus on securing government favours through lobbying efforts that grant them an unfair advantage over their competitors.

In the United States, the lobbying industry is a multibillion-dollar enterprise, with corporations spending vast sums of money to influence legislation and regulatory policy. According to data from OpenSecrets.org, the pharmaceutical industry alone spent over $300 million on lobbying in 2020, making it one of the most powerful and influential sectors in

Washington. The result of this lobbying is often favourable legislation, such as extended patent protections for drugs, which allow pharmaceutical companies to maintain monopolies and charge inflated prices for their products.

Lobbying also plays a significant role in securing government contracts. Defence contractors like Lockheed Martin, Boeing, and Raytheon spend millions of dollars each year lobbying Congress and the Pentagon to secure lucrative contracts for military equipment and services. These contracts, often awarded without competitive bidding, ensure that a small number of companies dominate the defence industry, with little incentive to innovate or reduce costs.

The influence of corporate lobbying extends beyond national governments to international organisations like the World Trade Organisation (WTO) and the International Monetary Fund (IMF). Through these institutions, multinational corporations can shape global trade policies in ways that protect their interests, often at the expense of smaller businesses and developing economies. For example, pharmaceutical companies have used their influence to push for stronger intellectual property protections in trade agreements, making it more difficult for developing countries to access affordable generic medicines.

The result of corporate lobbying is a distorted market where large, well-connected corporations enjoy privileged access to government resources and influence over policy. This not only undermines competition but also erodes public trust in the political system, as ordinary citizens see their interests sidelined in favour of corporate elites.

Globalist Strategies and the Sabotage of Free Markets

The examples above illustrate how crony capitalism distorts markets and suppresses competition. However, the influence of globalist agendas extends far beyond national borders, as powerful multinational corporations and supranational organisations work together to consolidate their control over the global economy.

Globalist strategies for undermining free markets typically involve the centralisation of power, the manipulation of financial systems, and the imposition of regulations that benefit established corporations while stifling innovation and competition. These strategies are designed to create a global economic order where a small group of elites controls the majority of resources and decision-making power, leaving ordinary people with little autonomy over their economic lives.

One of the key tools used by globalists to centralise economic control is the imposition of international trade agreements that prioritise corporate interests over national sovereignty and individual rights. These agreements, such as the Trans-Pacific Partnership (TPP) and the European Union's various trade agreements, often include provisions that allow corporations to sue governments for enacting laws that threaten their profits. This creates a system where multinational corporations can override the democratic will of the people, further entrenching their dominance in the global economy.

In addition to trade agreements, globalists use financial institutions like the International Monetary Fund (IMF) and the World Bank to impose austerity measures and structural adjustments on developing countries. These policies often include the privatisation of public assets, the reduction of social spending, and the deregulation of markets—all of which benefit multinational corporations at the expense of local businesses and communities.

Central banking also plays a crucial role in the globalist agenda. By controlling the money supply and manipulating interest rates, central banks can influence economic activity and create conditions that benefit the financial elite. For example, during the 2008 financial crisis, central banks around the world implemented policies such as quantitative easing, which flooded the financial system with cheap money. This artificially inflated asset prices, benefiting large financial institutions and wealthy investors, while doing little to help ordinary people recover from the economic downturn.

Conclusion: The Path Forward

The globalist hijacking of capitalism represents a profound distortion of the principles of free markets and individual enterprise. Through crony capitalism, multinational corporations and governments have created a system that rewards the powerful, entrenches monopolies, and stifles innovation and competition. This system benefits a small elite at the expense of the many, eroding economic freedom and undermining the potential for a truly free and prosperous society.

To reclaim capitalism from the grip of globalist agendas, it is essential to restore the principles of free markets, voluntary exchange, and individual responsibility. This requires not only reducing the influence of government in the economy but also dismantling the structures of crony capitalism that allow corporations to wield disproportionate power over markets and policy.

True capitalism—unfettered by state intervention and corporate collusion—offers the potential for genuine freedom, innovation, and prosperity. By rejecting crony capitalism and embracing the principles of a free-market society, individuals can reclaim their economic autonomy and build a future based on voluntary cooperation and mutual benefit.

Chapter 3:

The Globalist Agenda:

Towards a One-world Government

The Path to Global Governance

In recent decades, the push toward global governance has accelerated, fuelled by organisations that claim to represent the global community but often serve the interests of a small, powerful elite. Institutions like the International Monetary Fund (IMF), World Economic Forum (WEF), and the United Nations (UN) are increasingly shaping global policies that transcend national borders. These entities advocate for centralising power and authority in supranational structures, purportedly to address global challenges like economic inequality, climate change, and international security. However, a closer examination reveals a more troubling agenda—one aimed at reducing national sovereignty, eroding individual freedom, and advancing a form of technocratic rule that benefits global elites at the expense of ordinary people.

In this chapter, we will examine how globalist organisations pursue centralised governance under the guise of solving global issues, explore their stated goals versus their underlying agendas, and discuss the impact on local economies, individual autonomy, and national identity. We will also argue that these developments are part of a deliberate strategy to consolidate power in the hands of a global elite, with far-reaching consequences for national and personal freedom.

The Key Players: IMF, WEF, UN, and Beyond

Several key organisations are at the forefront of the globalist agenda. These institutions, often seen as benign or even necessary, exert significant influence over national governments, shaping policies that affect every aspect of society. Let us begin by examining the roles and stated objectives of some of the most prominent actors in the push toward global governance.

1. The International Monetary Fund (IMF)

The IMF was founded in 1944 with the aim of stabilising the global economy by providing financial assistance to countries in economic distress. Its stated goals include promoting global monetary cooperation, securing financial stability, facilitating international trade, and reducing poverty. While these goals may sound altruistic, the IMF has a long history of imposing strict economic policies, known as "structural adjustment programs," on countries that receive its loans.

These programs often involve austerity measures—cuts to public services, deregulation, and privatisation of state assets—that disproportionately affect the poor and working classes. The IMF's interventions have frequently led to social unrest, economic hardship, and a loss of national control over key industries. Moreover, the conditions attached to IMF loans often open the door to foreign corporations, which benefit from deregulated markets at the expense of local businesses and communities. Critics argue that the IMF serves the interests of multinational corporations and Western financial elites, rather than the countries it claims to help.

2. The World Economic Forum (WEF)

The WEF, founded in 1971, is an international organisation that brings together political leaders, business executives, academics, and activists to discuss global issues. Its annual meeting in Davos, Switzerland, is a gathering of the world's elite, where decisions about the future of global governance are made behind closed doors. The WEF promotes itself as a platform for addressing pressing global challenges such as climate change, inequality, and technological disruption. Its founder, Klaus Schwab, is also the architect of the "Great Reset" initiative, which aims to reshape the global economy in response to the COVID-19 pandemic.

The WEF's vision for the future involves a shift toward stakeholder capitalism, where corporations are seen as custodians of global public goods, such as the environment and social welfare. On the surface, this may seem like a positive development. However, in practice, stakeholder capitalism often translates into a greater concentration of power in the hands of corporate elites, who are not accountable to the public. The WEF's agenda also includes a push for digital transformation, with an emphasis on artificial intelligence, surveillance technologies, and the creation of digital currencies. These developments have profound implications for individual privacy, freedom, and economic independence, as they could lead to a world where personal data and financial transactions are controlled by a small group of tech companies and global financial institutions.

3. The United Nations (UN)

The United Nations, founded in 1945, is perhaps the most well-known globalist institution. Its mission is to promote peace, security, and cooperation among nations. While the UN has played a positive role in some areas, such as peacekeeping and humanitarian aid, its increasing influence over national governments has raised concerns about the erosion of national sovereignty.

The UN's Agenda 2030, also known as the Sustainable Development Goals (SDGs), is a blueprint for addressing global challenges such as poverty, inequality, and climate change. However, critics argue that the SDGs are a Trojan horse for global governance, as they give the UN and its affiliated organisations the authority to dictate national policies on a wide range of issues. For example, the UN's push for carbon reduction measures and environmental regulations often involves imposing top-down mandates on countries, with little regard for the unique needs and circumstances of individual nations. The result is a one-size-fits-all approach that undermines local control and ignores the voices of the people most affected by these policies.

Centralising Power: The Role of Trade Agreements and Supranational Institutions

One of the primary mechanisms through which globalists seek to centralise power is through trade agreements and supranational institutions that supersede national sovereignty. These agreements and institutions often operate behind closed doors, with little input from the public or elected representatives. They impose rules and regulations that restrict the ability of national governments to act in the interests of their own citizens, effectively transferring decision-making authority to global elites.

1. Trade Agreements that Supersede Sovereignty

Trade agreements like the Trans-Pacific Partnership (TPP) and the North American Free Trade Agreement (NAFTA) are often touted as tools for promoting economic growth and cooperation. However, these agreements frequently include provisions that allow multinational corporations to challenge national laws and regulations in international tribunals. For example, under the investor-state dispute settlement (ISDS) mechanism, corporations can sue governments for implementing policies that they claim harm their profits, even if those policies are designed to protect public health, the environment, or workers' rights.

This system undermines the democratic process by allowing corporations to bypass national courts and challenge the authority of elected governments. It also creates a chilling effect, as governments may be reluctant to implement policies that could lead to costly lawsuits from powerful corporations. In this way, trade agreements serve as a tool for global elites to impose their agendas on nations, while limiting the ability of ordinary citizens to influence the laws and regulations that govern their lives.

2. Supranational Institutions and the Erosion of National Sovereignty

In addition to trade agreements, supranational institutions such as the European Union (EU) and the World Trade Organisation (WTO) play a key role in the globalist agenda. These institutions are designed to facilitate cooperation between nations, but they often function as mechanisms for centralising power in the hands of unelected bureaucrats.

For example, the European Union has increasingly taken control over key areas of policy, such as trade, immigration, and environmental regulation, leaving member states with little autonomy over their own affairs. The EU's complex system of governance, with its unelected European Commission and opaque decision-making processes, has been criticised for being undemocratic and unaccountable to the people it claims to represent. The result is a system where decisions that affect millions of people are made by a small group of elites, with little input from the public.

Similarly, the World Trade Organisation sets global trade rules that member countries must follow, even if those rules conflict with national laws or the will of the people. The WTO has the authority to enforce its rulings through sanctions, further limiting the ability of national governments to act in the interests of their own citizens. This concentration of power in supranational institutions erodes national sovereignty and reduces the ability of individuals to influence the policies that govern their lives.

The Erosion of National Identity, Culture, and Individual Freedom

One of the most insidious effects of the globalist agenda is the erosion of national identity, culture, and individual freedom. As power is increasingly centralised in global institutions, the unique identities and traditions of nations and communities are being eroded, replaced by a homogenised global culture that serves the interests of a global elite.

1. The Erosion of National Identity and Culture

Globalist institutions often promote policies that prioritise global integration and multiculturalism over the preservation of national identity and cultural heritage. For example, the UN's Agenda 2030 emphasises the need for "inclusive and sustainable" societies, which often translates into policies that prioritise the needs of global migrants and international corporations over the interests of local communities. While diversity and inclusion are important values, the globalist agenda often goes further, pushing for a form of cultural homogenisation that undermines the unique identities and traditions of individual nations.

This erosion of national identity is particularly evident in Europe, where the EU's open borders policy has led to significant demographic and cultural changes in many countries. While immigration can bring economic benefits and cultural enrichment, the rapid pace of change has created social tensions and raised concerns about the loss of national identity. In many cases, local communities feel that their voices are being ignored as global elites impose policies that prioritise global integration over the preservation of cultural heritage.

2. The Loss of Individual Freedom and Autonomy

The globalist agenda also has profound implications for individual freedom and autonomy. As power is centralised in global institutions, individuals have less control over the decisions that affect their lives. Globalist policies often involve top-down mandates that limit personal freedom and impose uniform standards on diverse populations.

For example, the push for digital currencies and cashless societies, promoted by institutions like the IMF and the WEF, threatens to erode individual privacy and financial independence. Digital currencies, controlled by central banks, would allow governments and global institutions to monitor and control financial transactions, potentially limiting individuals' ability to make purchases or engage in economic activities without government oversight. This would give global elites unprecedented control over the financial system and the ability to restrict personal freedom in the name of security or economic stability.

The Globalist Endgame: A Deliberate Strategy to Reduce Individual Autonomy

The globalist agenda is not simply the result of well-meaning attempts to address global challenges. It is part of a deliberate strategy to consolidate power in the hands of a global elite, while reducing the autonomy of individuals and nations. By centralising power in supranational institutions, imposing top-down mandates, and promoting policies that erode national identity and individual freedom, globalists are creating a world where ordinary people have less control over their lives and fewer opportunities to shape their own destinies.

This concentration of power in the hands of a global elite is not a natural or inevitable outcome. It is the result of deliberate decisions made by powerful actors who benefit from the current system. The push for global governance, the erosion of national sovereignty, and the loss of individual freedom are all part of a broader strategy to create a world where a small group of elites holds the reins of power, while the rest of humanity is relegated to the role of passive subjects.

Conclusion: The Impact on Our Daily Lives

The globalist agenda may seem abstract and distant, but its effects are felt in every aspect of our daily lives. From the policies that shape our economies and the regulations that govern our businesses, to the erosion of privacy and the loss of national identity, globalism is reshaping the world in ways that affect us all. By understanding the true nature of the globalist agenda and its impact on our freedom and autonomy, we can begin to challenge the concentration of power in the hands of global elites and work toward a world where individuals and nations are free to determine their own destinies.

In the next chapter, we will explore how democracy, far from being a tool for empowerment, has become a mechanism for control, serving the interests of global elites rather than the people it claims to represent.

Chapter 4:

Democracy as a Mechanism of Control

The Democratic Ideal vs. The Democratic Reality

Democracy has long been hailed as the ultimate political system, one that reflects the will of the people and ensures that every voice is heard. Its promise of freedom, equality, and self-governance has inspired revolutions and movements around the world. In theory, it provides a structure where power is vested in the hands of the people, with leaders held accountable through elections, open debate, and the rule of law. However, the reality of modern democracy often falls far short of these ideals. In many contemporary democracies, especially in the West, elites—whether political, corporate, or financial—manipulate the system to maintain their power and control, rendering the democratic process a tool of oppression rather than empowerment.

This chapter delves into the ways democratic systems are subverted by elites, with particular attention to the influence of major corporations, tech companies, and financial institutions. We will examine how elections are influenced by money and media, how public policy is shaped through lobbying and political donations, and how the so-called democratic process often offers the illusion of choice. Finally, we will analyse how modern democracy has failed to protect individual freedoms, using specific case studies from different countries to highlight these failures.

The Manipulation of Democratic Systems by Elites

One of the central problems in contemporary democracies is that the systems designed to protect and represent the people are easily manipulated by powerful elites. These elites, composed of politicians, corporate leaders, and financial titans, have co-opted the democratic process to serve their interests. The mechanisms they use include corporate influence over elections, media propaganda, and the consolidation of power within political parties, which together undermine the legitimacy of democratic governance.

Corporate Influence over Elections

A fundamental feature of democracy is the idea that elections reflect the will of the people. However, in many democracies today, elections are increasingly determined by money. The role of corporate funding in elections, particularly in countries like the United States, has distorted the democratic process. The Supreme Court's 2010 ruling in Citizens United v. Federal Election Commission allowed corporations and unions to spend unlimited amounts of money on political campaigns, arguing that this was a matter of free speech. In reality, this decision opened the floodgates for corporate interests to dominate elections.

Corporations and wealthy individuals now spend billions of dollars to influence elections, making it nearly impossible for candidates who refuse corporate donations to compete. Political action committees (PACs) and Super PACs serve as conduits for funnelling vast sums of money into elections, ensuring that politicians who serve corporate interests are far more likely to succeed. As a result, the interests of multinational corporations—whether related to tax policies, deregulation, or labour laws—often take precedence over the needs and desires of ordinary citizens.

For example, the pharmaceutical industry in the United States is one of the largest contributors to political campaigns. Its influence on lawmakers has ensured that policies such as drug pricing reform are continually stalled, even as millions of Americans struggle with exorbitant healthcare costs. This manipulation of the electoral process illustrates how corporate money can overpower the will of the people in democratic systems.

Media Propaganda and the Shaping of Public Opinion

In addition to corporate money, media propaganda plays a crucial role in manipulating democratic outcomes. Major media outlets, often owned by powerful corporations or wealthy individuals, shape public opinion in ways that serve elite interests. By controlling the narrative, these media conglomerates ensure that only certain viewpoints are amplified, while others are marginalised or ignored.

For instance, during elections, media coverage tends to favour candidates who align with corporate interests. This is evident in the disparity between how populist candidates, who challenge the status quo, and establishment candidates, who support the existing power structures, are portrayed. Populist candidates are often depicted as radical, dangerous, or unelectable, while establishment candidates are framed as pragmatic, experienced, and safe. This media bias limits the scope of political debate and narrows the range of choices available to voters.

Moreover, media outlets often act as gatekeepers of information, focusing on sensationalist stories that drive ratings while ignoring critical issues like income inequality, climate change, or systemic corruption. The media's role in shaping public opinion ensures that the electorate is not fully informed about the true nature of the choices before them, making it easier for elites to maintain control.

The Role of Corporations, Tech Giants, and Financial Institutions

Beyond the manipulation of elections and media, major corporations, particularly in the tech and financial sectors, wield immense power over democratic processes. Through lobbying, political donations, and behind-the-scenes influence, these entities shape public policy to suit their interests, often at the expense of ordinary citizens.

Lobbying and Political Donations

Lobbying has become one of the most powerful tools used by corporations to influence public policy. In many democratic countries, lobbying is a multibillion-dollar industry, with corporations hiring armies of lobbyists to advocate for policies that serve their interests. In the United States, for example, the pharmaceutical, oil, and financial industries are among the top spenders on lobbying. These industries invest heavily in shaping legislation to ensure that regulations are favourable to their businesses.

One clear example of this is the financial sector's influence on deregulation. In the years leading up to the 2008 financial crisis, Wall Street banks spent millions of dollars lobbying for the repeal of regulations like the Glass-Steagall Act, which had been enacted to prevent financial speculation and protect consumers. The eventual repeal of this legislation allowed banks to engage in risky financial practices that ultimately led to the global financial meltdown. Even after the crisis, Wall Street continued to exert influence over lawmakers, ensuring that meaningful reform efforts, such as breaking up the big banks, were thwarted.

In Europe, corporate lobbying has also been a significant force. The European Union is often subject to intense lobbying from multinational corporations seeking to influence policies on trade, environmental regulation, and labour laws. This has led to a democratic deficit, where unelected bureaucrats, swayed by corporate interests, make decisions that affect millions of people across Europe.

Tech Companies and the Control of Information

In the digital age, tech giants like Google, Facebook, and Amazon have become some of the most powerful corporations in the world. Their control over vast amounts of data and information gives them unprecedented influence over public discourse, privacy, and even the outcomes of elections.

These tech companies wield their power in several ways. First, through their platforms, they control the flow of information. Social media algorithms, designed to maximise engagement and profit, prioritise sensationalist content, often at the expense of nuanced, fact-based discussion. This contributes to the polarisation of political discourse, as users are fed content that reinforces their existing views rather than exposing them to diverse perspectives.

Second, tech companies have significant political influence through lobbying and donations. In recent years, Silicon Valley has become a major player in

American politics, with tech CEOs contributing vast sums to political campaigns and funding think tanks that shape public policy. For example, in the 2020 U.S. election, tech executives were among the top donors to both major political parties, ensuring that their interests were represented regardless of the election's outcome.

Furthermore, tech companies often collaborate with governments to collect data on citizens, raising concerns about surveillance and the erosion of privacy. The Cambridge Analytica scandal, in which Facebook data was harvested to influence voter behaviour, is just one example of how tech companies can be used to manipulate democratic processes. The increasing reliance on digital platforms for political engagement has given these corporations enormous power to shape elections, public opinion, and policy.

Financial Institutions and Global Economic Policy

In addition to tech companies, financial institutions play a critical role in shaping democratic processes and public policy. Global financial institutions like the International Monetary Fund (IMF) and World Bank, as well as central banks like the Federal Reserve, exert immense influence over national economies. Their policies often prioritise the interests of multinational corporations and wealthy elites, while disregarding the needs of ordinary citizens.

For example, the IMF's structural adjustment programs, which are imposed on countries seeking financial assistance, often require the privatisation of public assets, cuts to social services, and deregulation. These policies disproportionately harm the poor and working-class, while benefiting multinational corporations that can exploit newly deregulated markets. In Greece, for instance, austerity measures imposed by the IMF and European Central Bank in the wake of the financial crisis led to widespread poverty, unemployment, and social unrest, while foreign investors profited from the privatisation of state assets.

At the same time, central banks like the Federal Reserve have enormous power to shape economic policy through interest rates, quantitative easing, and other monetary tools. These policies often benefit financial institutions and wealthy investors, while doing little to address systemic inequality. For example, the Federal Reserve's response to the COVID-19 pandemic included massive injections of liquidity into financial markets, which boosted stock prices and enriched the wealthy, even as millions of Americans lost their jobs and struggled to make ends meet.

The Illusion of Choice in Modern Democracies

One of the most insidious aspects of modern democracy is the illusion of choice. In many democratic systems, the options presented to voters are often limited to two or three political parties, all of which serve the interests of the same elites. This creates a situation where voters may feel they are participating in a meaningful democratic process, but in reality, their choices are constrained by the narrow range of policies offered by establishment parties.

The Convergence of Political Parties

In many democracies, particularly in the West, there has been a growing convergence between major political parties. Whether it's the Republican and Democratic parties in the United States or the Conservative and Labour parties in the United Kingdom, the differences between these parties on key economic and foreign policy issues have become increasingly marginal. Both sides of the political spectrum often support policies that benefit corporations, such as tax cuts for the wealthy, deregulation, and free trade agreements.

For example, both major U.S. political parties have consistently supported military interventions

abroad, despite public opposition. Similarly, both parties have been complicit in the deregulation of Wall Street, the expansion of mass surveillance programs, and the erosion of civil liberties in the name of national security. This convergence of interests between the political establishment and corporate elites ensures that regardless of which party is in power, the same neoliberal policies continue to dominate.

Case Studies: Failures of Democracy

The failure of democracy to protect individual freedoms and serve the people can be seen in several case studies around the world.

- The United States: Despite being one of the world's oldest democracies, the U.S. has seen a growing disconnect between the government and the people. From the influence of corporate money in elections to the erosion of civil liberties through mass surveillance programs like PRISM, American democracy has increasingly served the interests of elites rather than ordinary citizens.

- The European Union: The EU's democratic deficit is well-documented, with unelected bureaucrats in Brussels making decisions that affect millions of Europeans. The imposition of austerity measures on countries like Greece and Spain, despite widespread public opposition, highlights the disconnect between EU institutions and the will of the people.

- India: As the world's largest democracy, India faces significant challenges related to corruption, corporate influence, and the erosion of civil liberties. The rise of tech surveillance, coupled with corporate control over key industries, has led to growing concerns about the future of democracy in the country.

Conclusion: The Contradictions of Democracy in Practice

The gap between democratic ideals and the realities of state power and corporate control has never been wider. While democracy promises freedom, equality, and self-governance, the modern democratic process has been co-opted by elites who use it to maintain their control. Through corporate influence over elections, media propaganda, and the shaping of public policy by powerful institutions, democracy has become a mechanism of control rather than empowerment.

In the next chapter, we will explore how the illusion of choice within democratic systems masks the reality that both political options often serve the same elite interests, further eroding the ability of individuals to influence the direction of their societies.

Chapter 5:

The False Choice: Democracy vs. Totalitarianism

The prevailing narrative suggests that democracy and totalitarianism are diametrically opposed political systems. Democracy, characterised by popular sovereignty, limited government, and individual liberties, is often idealised as the pinnacle of human governance. Totalitarianism, on the other hand, is typically associated with authoritarian rule, suppression of dissent, and pervasive state control. However, a closer examination reveals that these two systems, despite their apparent differences, can converge towards similar outcomes, particularly in terms of state control and the erosion of individual freedoms.

The Illusion of Choice: Democracy and Totalitarianism as Two Sides of the Same Coin

The illusion of choice between democracy and totalitarianism is perpetuated by the belief that they represent fundamentally distinct ideologies. Democracy is often presented as the embodiment of freedom and progress, while totalitarianism is portrayed as a dystopian aberration. Yet, a careful analysis reveals that both systems can lead to strikingly similar results.

One of the key similarities between democracy and totalitarianism lies in their potential to concentrate power in the hands of a few. In democratic societies, power is ostensibly distributed among various institutions and individuals. However, over time, power can become increasingly concentrated in the hands of the executive branch, the bureaucracy, or powerful interest groups. This concentration of power can erode the checks and balances that are essential to a healthy democracy.

Similarly, totalitarian regimes, while characterised by a highly centralised and authoritarian form of government, can also exhibit elements of popular participation. For example, totalitarian leaders often seek to legitimise their rule through popular support, which can be achieved through propaganda, mass mobilisation, and the creation of a cult of personality. In this way, totalitarian regimes can manipulate public opinion to maintain their grip on power.

Western Democracies and the Erosion of Freedom

Western democracies have a long history of promoting freedom and individual rights. However, in recent decades, there has been a disturbing trend towards policies that are often associated with totalitarian regimes. Mass surveillance, state censorship, and coercive taxation are just a few examples of policies that have been implemented in Western democracies.

Mass surveillance programs, such as those employed by the United States and other Western countries, have raised serious concerns about privacy and civil liberties. These programs involve the widespread collection and analysis of personal data, including communications, location information, and online activities. Such surveillance can be used to monitor and control citizens, limiting their ability to express themselves freely and engage in political dissent.

State censorship is another area where Western democracies have increasingly adopted policies that resemble those of totalitarian regimes. Governments have sought to restrict access to information and control public discourse through a variety of means, including internet filtering, media regulation, and the suppression of dissenting voices. This erosion of freedom of speech and expression is a hallmark of totalitarian regimes.

Coercive taxation is another policy that can be used to control and manipulate citizens. By imposing heavy tax burdens, governments can extract wealth from individuals and corporations, reducing their economic independence and increasing their reliance on the state. This can lead to a situation where citizens feel powerless to resist the demands of the government, effectively creating a form of economic coercion.

The Convergence Towards Authoritarianism

The convergence between democracy and totalitarianism can be attributed to a number of factors. One of the most important factors is the concentration of power in the hands of a few. As power becomes more centralised, it becomes easier for those in positions of authority to exercise control over the population. This can lead to a gradual erosion of individual freedoms and the establishment of an authoritarian state.

Another factor that contributes to the convergence between democracy and totalitarianism is the increasing role of technology in modern societies. Technology can be used to monitor and control citizens, limiting their ability to express themselves freely and engage in political dissent. This can create a surveillance state that is indistinguishable from a totalitarian regime.

Finally, the erosion of trust in institutions can also contribute to the convergence between democracy and totalitarianism. When citizens lose faith in their government, they may be more willing to accept authoritarian rule as a means of restoring order and stability. This can create a fertile ground for the rise of authoritarian leaders and the establishment of a totalitarian regime.

The Myth of Democracy as the Only Alternative

The prevailing narrative suggests that democracy is the only viable alternative to totalitarianism. However, this is a false dichotomy. There are other political systems that can offer a more effective and just way of organising society.

One such alternative is anarcho-capitalism. Anarcho-capitalism is a political philosophy that advocates for the abolition of the state and the voluntary association of individuals. It is based on the principles of individual liberty, property rights, and free markets. Anarcho-capitalists argue that a society based on these principles would be more prosperous, peaceful, and just than one that relies on the coercive power of the state.

While anarcho-capitalism may seem radical to some, it offers a compelling vision of a society that is free from the tyranny of both democracy and totalitarianism. By rejecting the notion that the state is necessary for the provision of essential goods and services, anarcho-capitalists argue that individuals can create a more just and equitable society through voluntary cooperation and market exchange.

The belief that democracy and totalitarianism are fundamentally opposed systems is a myth. A closer examination reveals that these two systems can converge towards similar outcomes, particularly in terms of state control and the erosion of individual freedoms. Western democracies have increasingly adopted policies that are often associated with totalitarian regimes, such as mass surveillance, state censorship, and coercive taxation. This convergence towards authoritarianism is a result of the concentration of power, the increasing role of technology, and the erosion of trust in institutions.

The myth of democracy as the only alternative to totalitarianism must be challenged. Anarcho-capitalism offers a compelling vision of a society that is free from the tyranny of both democracy and totalitarianism. By rejecting the notion that the state is necessary for the provision of essential goods and services, anarcho-capitalists argue that individuals can create a more just and equitable society through voluntary cooperation and market exchange.

Chapter 6:

The Moral Case for Anarcho-Capitalism

Reimagining the Foundations of Society

The idea of anarcho-capitalism represents a radical departure from conventional political thought, envisioning a society where individual freedoms are paramount, and coercive institutions are dismantled. At its core, anarcho-capitalism advocates for a system of voluntary interactions grounded in ethical principles such as private property, the non-aggression principle, and the belief in free markets as the best means of human cooperation. This chapter will lay out the moral case for anarcho-capitalism, critiquing the state's coercive power and demonstrating that true freedom can only flourish in a society built upon voluntary associations.

We will examine how state power operates through coercion, taxation, and centralised authority, all of which violate individual freedoms. Historical precedents of decentralised societies that embody anarcho-capitalist principles will be explored, illustrating how such systems can thrive. Furthermore, we will highlight the troubling convergence of Western democracies toward authoritarianism through policies associated with totalitarian regimes—mass surveillance, state censorship, and coercive taxation. By dismantling the myth that democracy is the sole alternative to totalitarianism, we will present anarcho-capitalism as a viable third option that champions personal autonomy and ethical governance.

Ethical Principles of Anarcho-Capitalism

At the heart of anarcho-capitalism lies a set of ethical principles that provide a framework for understanding human interactions and governance. These principles include voluntary interactions, the protection of private property, and the non-aggression principle, all of which form the moral foundation of a truly free society.

1. Voluntary Interactions

Anarcho-capitalism posits that all human interactions should be voluntary and consensual. This principle recognises the inherent dignity and autonomy of individuals, advocating that people should engage in trade, cooperation, and association without coercion. The premise is simple: when individuals freely choose to engage in transactions or relationships, both parties benefit, leading to mutual prosperity and cooperation.

The moral superiority of voluntary interactions over coercive ones is evident in countless aspects of life, from business transactions to social relationships. In a truly free society, individuals would form contracts based on mutual consent, creating an environment where trust and cooperation flourish. This stands in stark contrast to state systems, where interactions are often dictated by laws and regulations imposed without the explicit consent of those affected.

2. Protection of Private Property

Private property is a cornerstone of anarcho-capitalist philosophy, viewed as an extension of individual rights and autonomy. The right to own and control property allows individuals to make decisions about their resources and engage in productive activities that contribute to societal wealth. Property rights provide incentives for innovation, investment, and responsible stewardship, enabling individuals to reap the rewards of their efforts.

The moral argument for private property is rooted in the principle of self-ownership. Individuals own themselves and, by extension, the fruits of their labour. The violation of property rights—whether through theft, taxation, or expropriation—constitutes a violation of individual freedom and dignity. Anarcho-capitalism advocates for a society where property rights are respected and protected, allowing individuals to flourish without interference from coercive entities.

3. The Non-Aggression Principle (NAP)

The non-aggression principle is a fundamental tenet of anarcho-capitalism, asserting that individuals should not initiate force or coercion against others. This principle establishes a clear moral boundary: while individuals are free to act and pursue their interests, they must do so without infringing on the rights of others. The NAP serves as a guiding ethical framework for interactions in a free society, promoting peaceful coexistence and cooperation.

The implications of the NAP are profound. In a society that respects this principle, disputes would be resolved through negotiation, arbitration, and voluntary agreements rather than through violence or state intervention. This promotes a culture of respect, accountability, and personal responsibility—values that are essential for a thriving society.

The Moral Critique of State Power

To understand the moral case for anarcho-capitalism, it is essential to critically assess the role of the state and its impact on individual freedoms. State power, by its very nature, relies on coercion, which fundamentally contradicts the ethical principles outlined above.

1. Coercion and the State

At its core, the state is a coercive institution that exercises authority over individuals and communities. It maintains power through the threat of violence, imposing laws and regulations that dictate how individuals must behave. This coercive nature inherently undermines the principles of voluntary interactions and individual autonomy.

The imposition of laws is often accompanied by punitive measures, including fines, imprisonment, and other forms of state-sanctioned violence. These actions violate the moral principle of consent, as individuals are compelled to comply with rules they may not agree with. The state's use of force to enforce compliance creates an environment of fear and distrust, hindering cooperation and social cohesion.

2. Taxation as Theft

One of the most egregious forms of state coercion is taxation. Taxes are not voluntary contributions but rather enforced levies that individuals must pay under threat of penalty. This practice constitutes a form of theft, as it involves the taking of individuals' hard-earned resources without their consent.

Taxation undermines individual freedom by redistributing wealth according to the state's priorities rather than allowing individuals to allocate their resources according to their own values and preferences. It discourages productivity and innovation, as individuals are less incentivised to work harder when a significant portion of their earnings is taken by the state. Furthermore, taxation often funds programs and policies that individuals may morally oppose, perpetuating a cycle of coercion and control.

3. Centralised Authority and the Erosion of Freedom

The centralisation of authority within state systems poses a significant threat to individual freedoms. As power becomes concentrated in the hands of a few, the potential for abuse and tyranny increases. Centralised authority often leads to the implementation of policies that infringe upon personal liberties and autonomy.

In many cases, governments justify the erosion of individual freedoms in the name of security, public health, or social welfare. However, these justifications often mask a deeper agenda of control and repression. The expansion of state power typically results in an increase in surveillance, censorship, and regulation, all of which serve to limit personal freedoms and stifle dissent.

Historical Precedents and Decentralised Societies

While the modern state is often viewed as the only viable model of governance, historical precedents exist that demonstrate the potential for anarcho-capitalist ideas to flourish in decentralised societies. These examples provide evidence that ethical governance can exist outside of state structures.

1. The Medieval Icelandic Althing

One of the earliest examples of a decentralised, stateless society can be found in medieval Iceland, where the Althing was established in 930 AD. The Althing served as an assembly for local chieftains to resolve disputes and make collective decisions without a formal government. Disputes were settled through arbitration, and individuals had the freedom to choose their legal representatives.

This system thrived for several centuries, demonstrating that a society could function effectively without a centralised authority. The voluntary nature of interactions, coupled with a respect for property rights and the resolution of conflicts through mutual consent, allowed the Icelandic community to prosper without the coercive mechanisms of a state.

2. The American Wild West

The American Wild West also offers a historical precedent for anarcho-capitalist principles in practice. In the absence of established law enforcement and government authority, communities developed their own systems of governance based on voluntary cooperation and mutual aid. Ranchers, miners, and settlers formed associations to protect their interests and resolve disputes, often relying on informal mechanisms of justice.

While the Wild West is often romanticised, it demonstrates that individuals can successfully self-organise and maintain order without the presence of a centralised state. The principles of personal responsibility and voluntary interactions were essential to the functioning of these communities.

3. Modern Examples of Decentralisation

In recent years, several modern examples of decentralisation have emerged, showcasing the potential for anarcho-capitalist ideas to thrive. Various grassroots movements, cooperatives, and local governance initiatives highlight the possibilities for self-organisation and voluntary cooperation.

For instance, the rise of blockchain technology and cryptocurrencies represents a shift towards decentralised systems that empower individuals to transact without reliance on traditional financial institutions. These technologies promote privacy, autonomy, and voluntary interactions, challenging the dominance of state-controlled currencies and financial systems.

Western Democracies and Authoritarianism

Despite the promise of democracy, many Western nations have increasingly adopted policies associated with authoritarian regimes, eroding individual freedoms and concentrating power in the hands of a few. This convergence towards authoritarianism calls into question the efficacy of democratic systems in protecting personal liberties.

1. Mass Surveillance

One of the most alarming trends in modern democracies is the rise of mass surveillance. Governments justify extensive surveillance programs as necessary for national security, often citing the threat of terrorism or crime. However, these measures violate individual privacy and erode trust in society.

Programs like the NSA's mass surveillance efforts reveal a disturbing reality: democratic governments are willing to sacrifice individual freedoms in the name of security. The normalisation of surveillance technologies creates a culture of monitoring, where citizens are constantly watched and their activities scrutinized.

2. State Censorship

In addition to surveillance, state censorship has become increasingly prevalent in democratic societies. Governments and powerful tech companies often collude to suppress dissenting voices, restricting access to information that challenges the dominant narrative. This is particularly evident in discussions around controversial topics such as climate change, public health policies, and social justice.

Censorship undermines the principles of free speech and open dialogue, essential components of a functioning democracy. The suppression of dissent not only stifles innovation and progress but also reinforces the control of elites over public discourse.

3. Coercive Taxation and Wealth Redistribution

Coercive taxation remains one of the most contentious issues in democratic societies, directly challenging the moral underpinnings of individual freedom and self-ownership. While proponents argue that taxation is necessary for funding public services and maintaining social welfare, the reality is that taxation functions as a tool of control, redistributing wealth according to state priorities rather than individual needs.

In many democratic nations, the tax system is highly progressive, imposing higher tax rates on wealthier individuals in an attempt to address income inequality. However, this form of wealth redistribution often leads to unintended consequences. The wealthy are incentivised to engage in tax avoidance strategies, diverting resources away from productive investments and entrepreneurial activities. This creates an environment of resentment and class warfare, pitting different segments of society against one another.

Moreover, the reliance on taxation to fund government programs can lead to an expanding state bureaucracy that grows ever more distant from the citizens it is supposed to serve. Bureaucrats, insulated from the consequences of their decisions, are incentivised to implement policies that may not reflect the desires or needs of the populace. This results in a disconnect between the government and the governed, further exacerbating feelings of disenfranchisement and powerlessness.

The Convergence Toward Authoritarianism

The cumulative effect of mass surveillance, state censorship, and coercive taxation in democratic societies creates an environment that increasingly resembles authoritarian regimes. While these democracies may maintain the façade of choice through electoral processes, the reality is that the options available to voters often serve the same elite interests, perpetuating the status quo and stifling genuine reform.

This convergence toward authoritarianism can be seen in various policy implementations that mirror those of totalitarian states:

1. Expansion of Police Powers: Governments frequently expand police powers in the name of public safety, leading to increased militarisation of law enforcement and a growing presence of armed officers in civilian life. This results in a culture of fear, where individuals may hesitate to exercise their rights for fear of state reprisal.

2. Legislation Against Dissent: In many democratic nations, laws have been enacted to criminalise dissenting voices, labelling protests and demonstrations as domestic terrorism. This chilling effect discourages public discourse and civic engagement, reinforcing the notion that questioning authority is inherently dangerous.

3. Erosion of Civil Liberties: The introduction of legislation like the Patriot Act in the United States and similar laws in other countries has eroded civil liberties in the name of security. These laws grant the state extraordinary powers to survey and detain individuals without due process, undermining the very principles of justice and freedom that democracies purport to uphold.

The Myth of Democracy as the Sole Alternative

One of the most pervasive myths perpetuated by proponents of state power is that democracy represents the only viable alternative to totalitarianism. These narrative paints a stark binary choice: participate in the democratic process or face the spectre of dictatorship. However, this oversimplification ignores the potential for a third option—anarcho-capitalism, which offers a truly liberating alternative grounded in ethical principles and individual autonomy.

Anarcho-capitalism rejects the notion that individuals must surrender their freedoms to a centralised authority in exchange for security and order. Instead, it advocates for a system where individuals voluntarily cooperate and trade, allowing for the organic emergence of social order without the need for coercive institutions. This framework aligns with the ethical principles of voluntary interactions, private property rights, and the non-aggression principle, offering a morally coherent alternative to both state control and authoritarianism.

Case Studies: Successful Anarcho-Capitalist Systems

To further illustrate the viability of anarcho-capitalist principles, we can draw on historical and contemporary examples where decentralised systems have flourished, demonstrating that societies can thrive without centralised authority.

1. Somalia's Stateless Period: Following the collapse of the Somali government in the early 1990s, the country experienced a period of statelessness. While often portrayed negatively in mainstream narratives, this time allowed for the emergence of informal markets and community-based governance structures. Without a central authority, various clans and local leaders assumed roles in providing security and resolving disputes, creating a semblance of order amidst chaos.

2. The Zapatista Movement in Mexico: The Zapatista movement in Chiapas, Mexico, embodies principles of self-governance and decentralisation. The Zapatistas

established autonomous communities that prioritise local decision-making and mutual aid over state intervention. Their focus on collective land ownership and participatory democracy illustrates the possibility of governance rooted in anarcho-capitalist principles.

3. Modern Cryptocurrency Ecosystem: The rise of cryptocurrencies and decentralised finance (DeFi) platforms exemplifies the potential of anarcho-capitalism in the digital age. These technologies facilitate peer-to-peer transactions without reliance on central banks or financial institutions, empowering individuals to control their wealth and engage in voluntary trade. The growing popularity of blockchain technology reflects a societal shift toward decentralisation and individual empowerment.

Toward a Free Society

The moral case for anarcho-capitalism is grounded in a profound respect for individual freedom, autonomy, and the belief that human beings are capable of self-organisation without coercive institutions. By prioritising voluntary interactions, the protection of private property, and the non-aggression principle, anarcho-capitalism offers a framework for ethical governance that aligns with our fundamental human rights.

The critique of state power highlights the dangers of coercion, taxation, and centralised authority, illustrating how these mechanisms violate individual freedoms and concentrate power in the hands of a few. As Western democracies increasingly adopt authoritarian policies reminiscent of totalitarian regimes, the need for an alternative vision of governance has never been more pressing.

Anarcho-capitalism emerges as a viable and moral alternative, advocating for a society where individuals are free to make choices, engage in voluntary exchanges, and build communities based on mutual consent. By dismantling the myth that democracy is the only option, we can envision a future where individual autonomy is celebrated, and coercive institutions are relegated to the past.

Philosophical Foundations of Anarcho-Capitalism

To ground the moral case for anarcho-capitalism in a robust philosophical framework, it is essential to draw upon the insights of influential thinkers who have articulated the principles of this ideology. Two prominent figures in the realm of anarcho-capitalist thought are Murray Rothbard and Lysander Spooner. Their contributions provide a solid foundation for understanding the ethical underpinnings of anarcho-capitalism and offer compelling critiques of state power.

Murray Rothbard: The Champion of Liberty

Murray Rothbard, a towering figure in libertarian and anarcho-capitalist thought, is perhaps best known for his advocacy of individual liberty and the non-aggression principle (NAP). Rothbard argued that all human interactions should be voluntary and free from coercion, positing that the initiation of force is inherently immoral. His work, particularly Man, Economy, and State and For a New Liberty, lays out a comprehensive vision for a society based on anarcho-capitalist principles.

1. The Non-Aggression Principle: Central to Rothbard's philosophy is the non-aggression principle, which asserts that aggression against another individual or their property is inherently wrong. This principle forms the moral bedrock of anarcho-capitalism, positioning the protection of individual rights as paramount. Rothbard argued that the state, by its very nature, engages in acts of aggression—through taxation, regulation, and coercion—thus violating the moral rights of individuals. In contrast, a society grounded in anarcho-capitalism respects the autonomy of individuals, allowing them to engage in peaceful interactions.

2. Critique of the State: Rothbard's critique of the state is particularly relevant in the context of this discussion. He argued that the state is not a neutral arbiter of justice but rather an institution that serves the interests of the powerful. By concentrating power in the hands of a few,

the state perpetuates inequality and undermines individual freedoms. Rothbard emphasised that individuals should be free to govern themselves through voluntary associations and private property rights, leading to a more just and equitable society.

3. Historical Context: Rothbard also explored historical precedents of anarcho-capitalism, highlighting instances where individuals organised themselves outside the purview of state control. He pointed to examples like the medieval Icelandic system of governance, which relied on decentralised dispute resolution mechanisms, demonstrating that order and cooperation can emerge in the absence of a centralised authority. This historical perspective challenges the prevailing narrative that only state control can provide social order and justice.

Lysander Spooner: The Radical Libertarian

Lysander Spooner was another pivotal figure whose writings laid the groundwork for anarcho-capitalist thought. An abolitionist, lawyer, and self-taught philosopher, Spooner's works such as No Treason: The Constitution of No Authority and The

Unconstitutionality of Slavery challenge the legitimacy of state power and advocate for individual sovereignty.

1. The Right to Self-Ownership: Spooner posited that each individual possesses an inherent right to self-ownership, a concept that is foundational to anarcho-capitalism. He argued that individuals are sovereign beings, entitled to govern themselves without interference from external authorities. This perspective aligns with the anarcho-capitalist emphasis on personal autonomy and the rejection of coercive systems of governance.

2. Critique of Government Legitimacy: Spooner famously asserted that the U.S. Constitution is invalid as a governing document because it relies on the consent of the governed—a consent that he argued had never been legitimately given. He believed that individuals are not bound by the laws of a government that they did not explicitly consent to, thereby rejecting the notion that democracy provides moral authority. This argument resonates with the anarcho-capitalist view that all forms of coercive governance lack legitimacy, reinforcing the need for voluntary and consensual interactions.

3. The Fallacy of Democracy: In his writings, Spooner critiqued the idea that democracy inherently leads to freedom. He argued that democratic systems often result in majority rule, which can oppress minority groups and infringe upon individual rights. This insight underscores the anarcho-capitalist perspective that democracy, rather than being a safeguard for liberty, can serve as a mechanism for control and oppression. By contrasting the fallibility of democratic systems with the ethical principles of anarcho-capitalism, Spooner's work highlights the need for a more decentralised approach to governance.

The Ethical Imperative for Anarcho-Capitalism

Drawing on the philosophical insights of Rothbard and Spooner, we can construct a compelling ethical case for anarcho-capitalism:

1. Voluntary Interactions: Anarcho-capitalism is rooted in the idea that all human interactions should be voluntary and consensual. The non-aggression principle

serves as a moral guideline, ensuring that individuals respect each other's rights and freedoms. This ethical framework fosters cooperation and harmony, promoting a society where individuals can flourish.

2. Rejection of Coercion: Both Rothbard and Spooner highlight the moral implications of coercion inherent in state power. Anarcho-capitalism provides a moral alternative that respects individual autonomy and allows for self-governance without the imposition of force. This rejection of coercion aligns with the broader philosophical tradition of liberalism, which values individual rights and personal freedom.

3. A Path to Justice: Anarcho-capitalism envisions a society where justice arises from voluntary associations rather than imposed authority. Rothbard's historical examples and Spooner's critiques of government legitimacy illustrate that decentralised systems can provide order and justice without the need for a centralised state. This vision emphasises the potential for community-based solutions and cooperative governance, challenging the narrative that only the state can provide social order.

A Philosophical Call to Action

In conclusion, the philosophical foundations of anarcho-capitalism, as articulated by thinkers like Murray Rothbard and Lysander Spooner, provide a robust ethical framework that supports the moral case for a society free from coercive institutions. By prioritising voluntary interactions, rejecting coercion, and envisioning a path to justice rooted in individual autonomy, anarcho-capitalism offers a compelling alternative to both state control and authoritarianism.

As we navigate the complexities of contemporary society, it is crucial to engage with these philosophical insights and consider the implications of anarcho-capitalism for our future. By recognising the inherent value of individual freedom and self-ownership, we can work toward a world that truly embodies the principles of justice, cooperation, and mutual respect. The challenge lies in reimagining our societal structures and advocating for a future where individuals are empowered to govern themselves, free from the chains of state control.

As we move forward, it is essential to foster discussions around these ideas, encouraging a re-evaluation of our societal structures and the possibility of a world built on the principles of anarcho-capitalism. Together, we can reclaim our individual sovereignty and create a society that truly embodies the ideals of freedom and cooperation.

Chapter 7:

Free Markets, True Freedom

The concept of the free market has long been celebrated as a cornerstone of economic prosperity and individual liberty. At its core, a free market is an economic system where the prices for goods and services are determined by unrestricted competition between privately owned businesses, without undue interference by the state. This contrasts sharply with crony capitalism, a system where governments and corporations collude to manipulate markets for their benefit, stifling competition and innovation. In this chapter, we will explore the distinctions between free markets and crony capitalism, and argue that true market freedom—achieved only in a stateless society—offers the best path toward equality, opportunity, and innovation.

Free Markets vs. Crony Capitalism

A truly free market is a system in which individuals and businesses are free to engage in voluntary exchanges without external coercion or artificial constraints. In this system, competition drives innovation, efficiency, and wealth creation. Entrepreneurs are free to enter the market, offer their goods and services, and compete on a level playing field. This openness allows for the constant flow of new ideas, technologies, and business models, benefiting society as a whole.

Crony capitalism, on the other hand, occurs when businesses and governments collaborate to create a market structure that benefits established firms at the expense of smaller competitors and consumers. In a crony capitalist system, corporations leverage their political connections to secure subsidies, favourable regulations, and barriers to entry that protect their market dominance. This manipulation of the market distorts competition, raises prices, and limits consumer choice. Instead of being driven by merit and innovation, success in a crony capitalist system is often determined by political favours and regulatory capture.

For example, in the United States, industries such as finance, pharmaceuticals, and energy are rife with examples of crony capitalism. Large banks receive government bailouts during financial crises, pharmaceutical companies benefit from regulatory monopolies and patent extensions, and energy companies lobby for subsidies and favourable regulations. These industries have become entangled with government, and as a result, their success is not solely the product of competition or consumer demand but is also shaped by political influence.

The Power of Free Markets to Foster Innovation and Progress

Free markets, when left to operate without heavy-handed regulation, have consistently demonstrated their capacity to drive innovation and create wealth. The most dynamic sectors of the global economy, such as technology and cryptocurrencies, have flourished in environments where regulation has been minimal. These industries provide compelling case studies of how free markets encourage innovation and competition.

1. The Technology Sector: Silicon Valley and the broader tech industry are often cited as prime examples of what can be achieved in a relatively free market environment. While governments have played a role in funding basic research, the tech industry's success has largely been driven by the ingenuity and risk-taking of individual entrepreneurs and companies. The lack of heavy regulation in the early stages of the tech industry allowed startups like Apple, Google, and Facebook to

emerge and disrupt established industries. The rapid pace of innovation in software development, digital communications, and e-commerce has transformed the global economy, creating new markets and opportunities for billions of people.

- Example: The App Economy: The creation of mobile app marketplaces by Apple and Google unleashed a wave of innovation and entrepreneurship. Developers from around the world were suddenly able to create apps and sell them to a global audience, leading to the emergence of new business models and industries. This explosion of creativity would not have been possible in a highly regulated market, where barriers to entry would have been insurmountable for many small developers. Today, the app economy generates billions of dollars in revenue and has created millions of jobs globally.

2. Cryptocurrencies and Decentralised Finance (DeFi): The rise of cryptocurrencies like Bitcoin and Ethereum, and the development of decentralised finance platforms, exemplify the potential of free markets to revolutionise traditional systems of exchange and finance. Cryptocurrencies emerged in response to the perceived failings of state-controlled monetary systems,

particularly in the aftermath of the 2008 financial crisis. The blockchain technology underlying cryptocurrencies enables secure, peer-to-peer transactions without the need for central authorities like banks or governments.

- Example: Bitcoin's Market-Driven Success: Bitcoin was created as a decentralised alternative to government-issued currencies. Its success is a testament to the power of market-driven innovation. Despite attempts by governments to regulate or restrict its use, Bitcoin has flourished as a store of value and a medium of exchange. The cryptocurrency market as a whole has grown to include thousands of coins and tokens, each competing for users and capital. The rise of decentralised finance (DeFi) platforms, which allow users to lend, borrow, and trade without intermediaries, is another example of how free markets foster financial innovation.

These examples highlight how industries can thrive when entrepreneurs are allowed to operate without the constraints of burdensome regulations. In these relatively free markets, competition encourages continuous innovation and improvement, benefiting consumers and the economy as a whole.

Free Markets, Equality, and Opportunity

One of the common criticisms of free-market capitalism is that it leads to inequality. However, this critique often conflates free markets with crony capitalism, where wealth is concentrated in the hands of those who can manipulate the political system to their advantage. In a truly free market, the competition would lead to greater equality of opportunity, as individuals are free to pursue their interests and compete on a level playing field.

In a free market, individuals are rewarded based on their ability to meet the needs and desires of consumers. This system encourages innovation and entrepreneurship, as anyone with a good idea and the willingness to take risks can succeed. The absence of state-enforced monopolies and barriers to entry ensures that the market remains open and dynamic, creating opportunities for upward mobility.

1. Small Business Growth: In a free market, small businesses and startups can compete with larger,

established firms without being hampered by excessive regulation or government favouritism. When governments intervene in the market, they often do so in ways that benefit large corporations, which can afford the costs of regulatory compliance, at the expense of smaller competitors. By removing these barriers, a free market creates an environment where small businesses can thrive, contributing to economic diversity and resilience.

2. Voluntary Exchange and Cooperation: Free markets are based on the principle of voluntary exchange, where individuals and businesses engage in mutually beneficial transactions. This system promotes cooperation and social harmony, as people are incentivised to work together to create value and meet each other's needs. In contrast to crony capitalism, where success is often determined by political connections, free markets reward those who are able to provide the best products and services at the best prices.

3. Creative Destruction and Innovation: Free markets encourage a process known as creative destruction, where outdated or inefficient industries and businesses are replaced by new and innovative ones. This process

ensures that resources are constantly being reallocated to their most productive uses, driving economic progress and improving living standards. In a regulated or state-controlled economy, this process is often stifled, as governments seek to protect established industries and jobs at the expense of innovation.

Stateless Societies and Market Freedom

A stateless society, free from the constraints of government intervention, would allow markets to operate in their purest form. Without the distortions caused by regulation, taxation, and government monopolies, individuals would be free to engage in voluntary exchanges and create wealth without interference.

1. Private Property and Contract Law: In a stateless society, private property rights would be respected, and individuals would be free to enter into contracts and agreements with one another. Dispute resolution and law enforcement could be handled by private arbitration firms, insurance companies, and community-based organisations, creating a competitive market for justice

and security services. This system would be more efficient and responsive to the needs of individuals than state-controlled legal systems, which are often slow, costly, and corrupt.

2. The Role of Reputation: In a stateless society, reputation would play a crucial role in regulating market behaviour. Businesses and individuals would be incentivised to act ethically and responsibly, as their success would depend on maintaining the trust of their customers and partners. In contrast to state-controlled economies, where regulations are often enforced unevenly or corruptly, market-driven mechanisms like reputation systems and consumer reviews would ensure accountability and transparency.

3. Decentralisation and Localism: A stateless society would likely be characterised by decentralisation and localism, as communities would be free to organise themselves according to their own preferences and values. This diversity would allow for a wide range of economic systems and social arrangements to coexist, creating a rich tapestry of experimentation and innovation. Without the need for a centralised authority, individuals would have greater freedom to choose the

type of community and economic system that best suits their needs.

Industries Thriving Under Minimal Regulation

Several industries have demonstrated the benefits of minimal regulation, providing further evidence that free markets lead to innovation, competition, and consumer choice.

1. Technology: The tech industry, particularly in its early days, operated with minimal government oversight. This freedom allowed companies like Apple, Microsoft, and Google to grow rapidly, creating new products and services that revolutionised entire industries. Today, the continued growth of technology companies, especially in areas like artificial intelligence and cloud computing, depends on maintaining a regulatory environment that allows for innovation.

2. Cryptocurrencies: As mentioned earlier, the cryptocurrency market is a prime example of an industry

that has thrived in the absence of heavy regulation. The decentralised nature of cryptocurrencies has allowed for the creation of a global financial system that operates independently of governments and central banks. This innovation would not have been possible in a heavily regulated market, where government-imposed barriers to entry would have stifled competition and creativity.

3. Sharing Economy: The rise of the sharing economy, exemplified by companies like Uber, Airbnb, and TaskRabbit, has been driven by the ability of individuals to engage in peer-to-peer transactions without significant government intervention. These platforms have created new markets for goods and services, providing consumers with more choices and better prices. While governments have attempted to regulate the sharing economy in some areas, its success has largely been due to the freedom of individuals to engage in voluntary exchanges.

True Freedom in Free Markets

In this chapter, we have explored the distinction between free markets and crony capitalism, highlighting how the latter distorts competition and limits innovation. We have also provided real-world examples of industries that have thrived under minimal regulation, demonstrating the power of free markets to drive progress and create opportunity. Finally, we have argued that a stateless society would allow for true market freedom, enabling individuals to engage in voluntary exchanges without interference from governments or corporations.

Free markets offer a path to true freedom, where individuals are free to pursue their interests, compete on a level playing field, and create wealth without coercion. By rejecting the distortions of crony capitalism and embracing the principles of voluntary exchange and competition, we can create a more just, equal, and prosperous society.

Chapter 8:

The Globalist Endgame: Surveillance, Central Banks, and Control

Chapter 7: The Globalist Endgame: Surveillance, Central Banks, and Control

In recent years, we have seen a dramatic shift in how global elites exert control over populations. Technologies once thought to enhance freedom and democracy—such as digital currencies, surveillance systems, and financial institutions—are increasingly being used to monitor, control, and suppress individual autonomy. The globalist agenda, embodied in the actions of central banks, governments, and international institutions, seeks to centralise power and strip individuals of their privacy and financial independence. In this chapter, we will analyse how surveillance technologies, central banking, and digital currencies play key roles in this globalist endgame, and how anarchy-capitalism provides a viable alternative through decentralisation and voluntary exchange.

The Rise of Surveillance Technologies

Surveillance technology has evolved at an unprecedented rate in the digital age. Governments and corporations now have the ability to track, monitor, and record nearly every aspect of a person's life. From smartphone data to social media activity, from facial recognition software to biometric identification systems, the tools of surveillance have been embedded into daily life. This surveillance infrastructure is not merely a tool for improving national security or public safety, as its proponents often claim. Rather, it is a mechanism for global control, one that erodes privacy and stifles dissent.

1. Mass Surveillance in the Digital Age: The revelations by whistleblowers such as Edward Snowden exposed the extent of global mass surveillance. Governments, particularly the United States through the NSA's PRISM program, have engaged in mass collection of data from phone calls, emails, and internet activity, often without judicial oversight or the knowledge of citizens. This mass surveillance apparatus allows governments to not only monitor threats to national security but also to track and manipulate political dissent, social movements, and individual behaviour.

2. Social Credit Systems and Digital Control: Perhaps the most overt manifestation of globalist surveillance is China's social credit system. Under this system, citizens are scored based on their behaviour—both online and

offline—with rewards and punishments meted out depending on their score. "Bad behaviour," such as criticising the government or associating with dissidents, results in penalties such as travel restrictions, denial of loans, or loss of employment opportunities. While China's system is the most extreme, Western governments are increasingly looking to adopt similar forms of digital control through surveillance technologies that monitor citizens' behaviour.

3. Tech Companies and Government Partnerships: Major technology companies like Google, Facebook, and Amazon have grown so large that they now operate as de facto extensions of state power. These companies collect massive amounts of personal data and, in many cases, share this data with governments or use it to shape public opinion. For example, social media platforms have become tools for controlling the flow of information, often censoring political speech that threatens the status quo. The collaboration between tech giants and governments accelerates the erosion of individual privacy and allows elites to manipulate public discourse.

The primary threat posed by surveillance technologies is their ability to create a population that is constantly watched and controlled. Fear of surveillance can stifle free speech, suppress political activism, and reduce the willingness of individuals to engage in dissenting activities. In this environment, the idea of privacy—once considered a fundamental right—is now being reframed as a privilege that can be revoked by the state.

Central Banks: The Engine of Global Control

At the heart of the globalist agenda is the power wielded by central banks. Institutions like the Federal Reserve, the European Central Bank, and the International Monetary Fund (IMF) have become the architects of modern monetary policy, controlling the flow of money, manipulating interest rates, and shaping the global economy. While central banks are often presented as neutral institutions tasked with ensuring financial stability, their role in consolidating power and controlling populations cannot be overstated.

1. The History of Central Banking: Central banks were originally established to stabilise national economies and provide a lender of last resort during financial crises. Over time, however, central banks have gained

extraordinary power, effectively becoming the sole authorities on monetary policy. The creation of the Federal Reserve in 1913 marked a turning point in American economic history, as it transferred the control of money supply from the public to a centralised, unelected body. This transfer of power allowed for unprecedented levels of financial manipulation, culminating in the ability of central banks to create money out of thin air through mechanisms such as quantitative easing.

2. The Consequences of Centralised Monetary Policy: Central banking allows elites to manipulate the economy in ways that benefit the wealthy while leaving the average citizen to bear the costs. For example, when central banks engage in quantitative easing (printing money to buy government bonds or other assets), the newly created money flows primarily to financial markets, inflating the prices of stocks and real estate. This benefits the wealthy, who own the majority of financial assets, while devaluing the purchasing power of the average citizen. In addition, central banks' control over interest rates can create asset bubbles, lead to unsustainable levels of debt, and exacerbate economic inequality.

- Example: The 2008 Financial Crisis and Bailouts: During the 2008 financial crisis, central banks around the world stepped in to bail out failing banks and financial institutions. The Federal Reserve, for instance, injected trillions of dollars into the banking system, while the U.S. government implemented a bailout package to save "too big to fail" institutions like AIG and Goldman Sachs. While the financial elite were rescued, millions of ordinary citizens lost their homes, jobs, and savings. The actions of central banks during this crisis revealed their true purpose: to protect the interests of the global financial elite at the expense of the broader population.

3. Central Bank Digital Currencies (CBDCs): One of the most concerning developments in recent years has been the push for Central Bank Digital Currencies (CBDCs). CBDCs are digital versions of fiat currencies that would be issued and controlled directly by central banks. While proponents argue that CBDCs could streamline payments and reduce the need for physical cash, the true purpose of these currencies is to provide central banks with greater control over individual financial transactions.

- Surveillance Through CBDCs: Unlike cash, which allows for anonymous transactions, CBDCs would be fully traceable and programmable. Central banks would have the ability to track every transaction in real-time, giving them unprecedented insight into individuals' financial lives. This surveillance power could be used to control how people spend their money, restrict purchases of certain goods, or even penalise individuals for engaging in politically undesirable behaviour. Moreover, CBDCs could be programmed to expire after a certain period, forcing individuals to spend their money rather than save it, further eroding financial independence.

Digital Currencies and the Quest for Financial Independence

In response to the growing power of central banks and the erosion of financial privacy, decentralised digital currencies like Bitcoin have emerged as a potential solution. These cryptocurrencies operate outside of the control of governments and central banks, offering individuals a means of exchange that is both private and secure.

1. The Philosophy of Bitcoin: Bitcoin was created in the aftermath of the 2008 financial crisis as a decentralised alternative to government-issued currencies. Its creator, known only by the pseudonym Satoshi Nakamoto, designed Bitcoin to operate without the need for a central authority. Bitcoin's decentralised ledger, known as the blockchain, allows for secure, peer-to-peer transactions without the need for intermediaries like banks or payment processors. This decentralisation makes it difficult for governments to control or censor transactions, giving individuals greater financial autonomy.

2. The Threat to Central Bank Control: Cryptocurrencies like Bitcoin and Ethereal pose a direct threat to the power of central banks. By providing individuals with an alternative to government-issued money, these digital currencies undermine the monopoly that central banks have over the money supply. Moreover, because cryptocurrencies operate on decentralised networks, they are resistant to censorship and government interference. This has made them popular among individuals seeking to escape the control of authoritarian regimes or evade oppressive financial regulations.

- Example: Bitcoin's Role in Economic Freedom: In countries like Venezuela and Zimbabwe, where hyperinflation has rendered government-issued currencies practically worthless, citizens have turned to Bitcoin as a store of value and a means of transacting outside of the government's control. By using cryptocurrencies, individuals in these countries have been able to preserve their wealth and maintain access to goods and services, even as their national economies collapse.

The Globalist Agenda: Eroding Privacy and Financial Independence

The globalist agenda, as embodied by the actions of central banks, governments, and international institutions, seeks to erode individual privacy and financial independence. Surveillance technologies allow governments to monitor and control the behaviour of their citizens, while central banks manipulate monetary policy to benefit the financial elite. The push for Central Bank Digital Currencies represents the next phase in this agenda, as it would grant governments even greater control over individuals' financial lives.

1. The Erosion of Privacy: As surveillance technologies become more sophisticated, individuals are losing the ability to live their lives without being constantly monitored. The combination of digital surveillance and financial control allows governments and corporations to track every aspect of a person's behaviour, from their spending habits to their political beliefs. This loss of privacy has profound implications for individual freedom, as it enables those in power to manipulate and control populations with unprecedented precision.

2. The Loss of Financial Independence: Central banks and governments are working to create a world where individuals have no financial autonomy. Through policies like quantitative easing, interest rate manipulation, and the promotion of digital currencies, central banks are consolidating control over the global economy. The result is a system in which individuals are increasingly dependent on the state for their financial well-being, with little ability to protect their wealth or resist government control.

Anarcho-Capitalism: A Decentralised Solution

Anarcho-capitalism offers a compelling alternative to the globalist agenda. By advocating for the elimination of the state and the decentralisation of power, anarcho-capitalism provides a framework for restoring individual autonomy and protecting privacy and financial

independence. In a stateless society, individuals would be free to engage in voluntary exchanges, create their own currencies, and establish private systems of governance.

1. Decentralised Currencies and Financial Freedom: In an anarcho-capitalist society, currencies would be created and maintained by private individuals or organisations, rather than by central banks. These decentralised currencies, such as Bitcoin, would allow individuals to transact freely without the need for government oversight or interference. Moreover, because these currencies operate on decentralised networks, they would be resistant to inflation, manipulation, and censorship, providing individuals with true financial independence.

2. Voluntary Associations and Privacy Protection: In the absence of a centralised state, individuals would be free to form voluntary associations to provide for their own security, governance, and dispute resolution. These associations would operate on the basis of mutual consent, rather than coercion, and would be subject to competition, ensuring that they serve the interests of their members. By decentralising power in this way, anarcho-capitalism offers a solution to the problem of mass surveillance and the erosion of privacy.

Conclusion: Reclaiming Autonomy Through Decentralization

The globalist endgame is clear: through the use of surveillance technologies, central banking, and digital currencies, elites seek to centralise power and control over individuals' lives. The erosion of privacy and financial independence is not an unfortunate side effect of these policies—it is their intended outcome. However, anarcho-capitalism provides a path forward. By embracing decentralisation, voluntary exchange, and private currencies, individuals can reclaim their autonomy and resist the control of global elites.

In the next chapter, we will explore how anarcho-capitalism's principles can be applied to create a more just, equal, and free society, where individuals are empowered to pursue their own interests without interference from the state or corporations.

Chapter 9:

Anarcho-Capitalism: A Vision for the Future

Imagine a world where governments no longer monopolise power, where individuals are free to live their lives without the constant interference of the state. A world where people, through voluntary interaction and mutual cooperation, create systems of governance, law, and security that serve their true interests. This is the world that anarcho-capitalism envisions: a society free from coercion, centralised control, and bureaucratic inefficiency, where individuals are empowered to take responsibility for their own well-being and prosperity.

In this chapter, we will explore how a future organised around anarcho-capitalist principles could function. We'll examine how governance, law, and security would work in the absence of a state, showing that many of the essential services we rely on today can be provided through voluntary means, often more efficiently and ethically. Additionally, we'll explore how technological advancements could facilitate the transition to such a society, offering a glimpse into a world where decentralised systems flourish and human potential is fully realised.

Governance Without the State: Decentralised Communities

In an anarcho-capitalist society, there would be no centralised government wielding monopoly power over individuals. Instead, governance would be organised around voluntary, decentralised communities that operate based on mutual consent. Each individual or group would have the freedom to form or join the community that best aligns with their values and preferences. These communities, in turn, would provide services such as law, security, and infrastructure on a voluntary basis.

1. Private Law Systems: In the absence of the state, law would be provided by competing private institutions. These institutions—private courts, arbitration agencies, and legal service providers—would be funded by individuals and businesses seeking fair and efficient resolution of disputes. Because these legal institutions would compete for customers, they would have a strong incentive to offer high-quality services, uphold contractual agreements, and ensure justice is served.

- Example: Private Arbitration: Private arbitration is already a common practice in today's world. Corporations and individuals often choose private arbitrators to resolve disputes because these systems tend to be faster, more efficient, and less costly than government-run courts. In an anarcho-capitalist society, arbitration would be the primary means of settling disputes, with competing arbitration firms offering specialised services tailored to the needs of different clients. If a particular arbitration firm develops a reputation for corruption or bias, it would lose business, giving all firms a strong incentive to maintain impartiality and fairness.

2. Decentralised Governance: Anarcho-capitalist societies would be organised into decentralised, self-governing communities. These communities could be based on geography, profession, religion, or any other shared interest. Each community would establish its own rules and norms, with membership entirely voluntary. Some communities might choose to implement traditional systems of governance, while others might experiment with new forms of decision-making. The key principle is that no single authority would have the power to impose its will on others; individuals would always be free to exit a community and join another that better suits their preferences.

- Example: Special Economic Zones: Special economic zones (SEZs) already offer a glimpse into how decentralised governance could work. These zones operate with their own set of rules and regulations, often distinct from the broader legal framework of the country they are in. In many cases, SEZs are more economically prosperous because they operate with fewer restrictions and lower taxes, attracting businesses and innovation. In an anarcho-capitalist future, entire communities could operate like SEZs, providing diverse governance structures and fostering competition between different approaches.

Security Without the State: Private Protection and Community Policing

One of the most frequently asked questions about anarcho-capitalism is how security would be maintained without a state. In the absence of government-controlled police forces, anarcho-capitalism proposes that security services be provided by private companies and community-based organisations. This model already exists in some capacity today, and with advancements in technology and increased competition, private security would likely become more efficient, more accountable, and more responsive to individual needs.

1. Private Security Companies: Private security firms would replace the monopoly on force currently held by state police. These firms would be hired by individuals, businesses, or communities to provide protection, investigate crimes, and respond to emergencies. Just like any other service provider in a free market, these companies would be incentivised to offer high-quality services because their reputation and revenue depend on customer satisfaction.

- Example: Private Security in Practice: Today, many businesses and wealthy individuals already rely on private security services to protect their properties and ensure safety. From gated communities to private investigators, private security often supplements or even replaces public police forces. In an anarcho-capitalist world, these services would expand, becoming available to everyone, not just the wealthy. Because there would be competition between security firms, they would be more likely to act ethically and responsibly, unlike state police forces, which often face little accountability.

2. Community Policing and Mutual Aid: Not all security would need to be outsourced to private firms. In an anarcho-capitalist society, communities could organise their own security through mutual aid networks and neighbourhood watch programs. These systems would rely on voluntary cooperation between members of the community to monitor and address safety concerns. By decentralising security, communities could tailor their protection efforts to meet local needs, fostering stronger relationships and a greater sense of personal responsibility.

 - Example: Community-Based Policing: In many parts of the world, informal community policing already plays a crucial role in maintaining order. For example, in some rural areas, where state police forces are absent or ineffective, local residents band together to provide mutual protection and resolve disputes. These systems are often based on long-standing traditions of cooperation and trust, demonstrating that communities can manage security effectively without the need for state intervention.

Law Without Coercion: The Role of Private Arbitration and Customary Law

One of the most important functions of any society is the enforcement of contracts and the resolution of disputes. In an anarcho-capitalist future, private arbitration and customary law would replace state-controlled courts. These systems would be voluntary, competitive, and based on mutual agreement, providing individuals with a more flexible and responsive legal framework.

1. Private Arbitration as a Legal System: Arbitration has proven to be an effective alternative to state courts in many sectors, from international business disputes to labour conflicts. In an anarcho-capitalist society, private arbitration agencies would offer specialised legal services tailored to the needs of their clients. Individuals and businesses would have the freedom to choose which arbitration agency to use, ensuring competition and accountability within the legal system.

   - Example: Historical Precedents of Private Law: The idea of private law is not new. In medieval Iceland, for example, the legal system was entirely privatised.

Disputes were resolved by arbitrators chosen by the parties involved, and laws were enforced by private individuals. Similarly, in Anglo-Saxon England before the Norman Conquest, customary law was enforced by local communities rather than a centralised state. These examples show that private, voluntary legal systems have functioned effectively in the past and could do so again in the future.

2. Customary Law and Contractual Agreements: In a decentralised society, laws would emerge organically through voluntary agreements and longstanding customs. Customary law is a system of rules that develops over time based on the behaviour and expectations of a community. Unlike state-imposed laws, which are often arbitrary and rigid, customary law reflects the real needs and preferences of the people who live under it. In an anarcho-capitalist future, communities would develop their own sets of customary laws, allowing for a more adaptable and responsive legal system.

- Example: The Law Merchant: During the medieval period, merchants across Europe developed a system of customary law known as the "Law Merchant" to regulate trade and resolve disputes. This legal framework operated independently of state control and was enforced through voluntary agreements between merchants. The Law Merchant allowed for the smooth functioning of international trade, demonstrating that private legal systems can be effective even in complex, large-scale economies.

Technological Advancements and the Future of Decentralization

Technological advancements are already paving the way for a decentralised future. Innovations in blockchain technology, smart contracts, and peer-to-peer networks have the potential to revolutionise how society is organised, making it easier than ever to replace state functions with voluntary, decentralised alternatives.

1. Blockchain Technology and Decentralised Governance: Blockchain technology provides a secure, transparent way to record transactions and agreements without the need for a central authority. In an anarcho-capitalist society, blockchain could be used to create decentralised systems of governance, where rules and agreements are enforced through cryptographic code

rather than coercive state power. For example, smart contracts—self-executing agreements that run on blockchain—could replace traditional legal contracts, automatically enforcing the terms agreed upon by the parties involved.

  - Example: Decentralised Autonomous Organisations (DAOs): DAOs are organisations that operate through blockchain-based smart contracts, allowing for decentralised decision-making and governance. Members of a DAO can vote on proposals, allocate resources, and enforce rules without the need for a centralised leader. In an anarcho-capitalist future, DAOs could be used to create decentralised communities, businesses, and even legal systems, giving individuals more control over the institutions they participate in.

2. Peer-to-Peer Networks and Economic Freedom: Peer-to-peer (P2P) networks allow individuals to exchange goods, services, and information directly with one another, without the need for intermediaries like governments or corporations. These networks are already being used to create decentralised marketplaces, where individuals can trade directly with one another using cryptocurrencies like Bitcoin. In an anarcho-

capitalist society, P2P networks would form the backbone of the economy, allowing individuals to engage in voluntary exchange free from state regulation and interference.

- Example: Cryptocurrency and Financial Independence: Cryptocurrencies

like Bitcoin and Ethereum are prime examples of how P2P networks can empower individuals by giving them control over their own finances. Unlike fiat currencies, which are controlled by central banks, cryptocurrencies operate on decentralised networks that are resistant to censorship and manipulation. In an anarcho-capitalist society, these decentralised currencies would replace government-issued money, giving individuals true financial independence.

The Future of Freedom: A Utopian Vision

The vision of anarcho-capitalism is not just a theoretical exercise—it is a practical blueprint for a future where individuals are free to live their lives without the coercive interference of the state. In this world, governance, law, and security would be provided by voluntary, competitive institutions that serve the needs of their customers rather than the interests of the powerful. Technological advancements would facilitate this transition, making it easier than ever for individuals to organise their own lives, communities, and economies in ways that align with their values and preferences.

Far from the chaos and disorder that critics often associate with the absence of a state, anarcho-capitalism offers a vision of true freedom, where individuals are empowered to take responsibility for their own well-being and protection. By embracing decentralisation, voluntary exchange, and private systems of governance, we can build a more just, equal, and free society—one where the coercive power of the state is replaced by the voluntary cooperation of individuals working together for mutual benefit.

In the next chapter, we will explore how these principles can be applied to specific industries and sectors, demonstrating the practical benefits of anarcho-capitalism in action. From healthcare to education to infrastructure, anarcho-capitalism offers real-world solutions that empower individuals and communities while eliminating the inefficiencies and injustices of state control. The future of freedom is within our reach, and it starts with embracing the principles of anarcho-capitalism today.

Chapter 10:

Conclusion: Reclaiming Individual Sovereignty

In a world dominated by centralised control, bureaucratic overreach, and political manipulation, the idea of individual sovereignty often feels like a distant, unattainable ideal. Yet, the purpose of this book has been to lay bare the flaws of the current system and present a compelling alternative—anarcho-capitalism. Throughout the preceding chapters, we have explored the shortcomings of democracy, exposed the insidious nature of globalist agendas, and made the case for a stateless society rooted in voluntary cooperation, free markets, and individual freedom.

The argument is simple but powerful: democracy, as it is practiced today, is not a system of freedom. It is a system that centralises power in the hands of elites, often under the guise of serving the public, but ultimately reinforcing crony capitalism and globalist interests. Global institutions and governments conspire to create monopolies, control financial systems, and erode individual autonomy. Through surveillance, taxation, and regulation, they strip away personal freedoms bit by bit, all while convincing the masses that their power is legitimate and necessary.

Anarcho-capitalism, by contrast, offers a different path —one where voluntary exchange, decentralisation, and private property are the guiding principles of society. It envisions a world where governance is not imposed from above by coercive states but emerges naturally from the voluntary cooperation of individuals. Law, security, and economic regulation are no longer monopolised by the state, but handled by private organisations and decentralised communities competing in a free market. This chapter will summarise the central arguments made in the book and provide a call to action for readers who wish to reclaim their individual sovereignty and embrace the principles of anarcho-capitalism in their own lives.

The Failures of Democracy

At the heart of this book is a critique of democracy as it is practiced today. While the ideal of democracy— government of, by, and for the people—remains appealing, the reality is far removed from this utopian vision. Instead of empowering individuals, modern democratic systems concentrate power in the hands of a select few, often operating at the behest of corporate and financial elites. Elections are less about genuine representation and more about manipulating public opinion to serve the interests of the powerful.

1. Corporate Influence Over Politics: Major corporations and financial institutions shape public policy through lobbying, campaign donations, and backroom deals, ensuring that elected officials prioritise their interests over the needs of the broader population. This is evident in countless examples of policies that disproportionately benefit large corporations, from tax breaks and subsidies to government bailouts. As discussed in earlier chapters, the political system has been co-opted by the very forces it claims to regulate.

2. The Illusion of Choice: Modern democracy offers the illusion of choice, where voters are given two or more political options, but all major candidates serve the same entrenched interests. Whether left or right, conservative or progressive, the underlying structure of power remains unchanged. The result is a perpetual cycle of dissatisfaction, where voters alternate between parties, hoping for meaningful change that never comes.

3. Democracy's Moral Failure: From a moral perspective, democracy is built on the premise of majority rule, which inevitably means that the rights of individuals can be overridden by the collective will. This leads to policies that infringe upon personal freedom and property rights, all justified in the name of "the greater good." Anarcho-capitalism rejects this notion, arguing instead for a society where individual rights are inviolable and where all interactions are based on voluntary consent rather than coercion.

Globalism: The March Toward Centralised Control

While democracy has failed to protect individual sovereignty at the national level, globalism presents an even greater threat. As discussed in previous chapters, globalist institutions such as the International Monetary Fund (IMF), World Economic Forum (WEF), and United Nations (UN) are working to centralise power on a global scale, eroding national sovereignty and imposing a one-size-fits-all approach to governance. These institutions claim to promote stability, development, and cooperation, but their true agenda is control.

1. Centralisation of Power: Globalist organisations and supranational institutions are increasingly undermining national governments, forcing countries to adopt policies dictated by unelected bureaucrats. Trade agreements, international regulations, and financial aid programs are often tools for coercion, compelling nations to sacrifice their autonomy in exchange for global approval or economic benefits. The end goal of this agenda is the creation of a centralised global authority that dictates policies for the entire world, with little regard for the unique needs or desires of individual countries or communities.

2. Erosion of Cultural Identity: One of the consequences of globalism is the erosion of national identity, culture, and traditions. Globalist policies often promote homogenisation, where local customs, values, and ways of life are sacrificed in favour of a universal set of standards. This erasure of cultural diversity is not merely a byproduct of globalist agendas but a deliberate strategy to make populations more malleable and easier to control. Anarcho-capitalism, by contrast, celebrates diversity and decentralisation, allowing communities to retain their unique identities while interacting with others on a voluntary basis.

3. The Surveillance State: A key component of the globalist agenda is the rise of the surveillance state, where governments and corporations track and monitor individuals' every move. From mass surveillance programs to the growing use of facial recognition technology, globalist institutions are working hand-in-hand with tech companies to create a world where privacy is a thing of the past. In such a system, dissent is easily crushed, and individuals are left with little recourse to defend their freedoms.

The Case for Anarcho-Capitalism

In response to the failures of democracy and the growing threat of globalism, this book has argued for anarcho-capitalism as the moral and practical alternative. Anarcho-capitalism is rooted in the belief that individuals have the right to live free from coercion, that private property is sacred, and that voluntary interactions —not state intervention—are the key to a prosperous and just society.

1. The Non-Aggression Principle (NAP): At the heart of anarcho-capitalism is the non-aggression principle, which holds that no individual or group has the right to initiate force against others. This principle stands in stark contrast to the state, which relies on coercion—through taxation, regulation, and enforcement of laws—to maintain control. An anarcho-capitalist society would be one where all interactions are voluntary, where individuals are free to pursue their own interests as long as they do not infringe on the rights of others.

2. Free Markets and Competition: Anarcho-capitalism promotes free markets, where businesses and individuals compete to provide goods and services without government interference. In such a system, the best ideas and innovations rise to the top, while inefficiency and corruption are weeded out through competition. This is in stark contrast to crony capitalism, where corporations rely on government favouritism and bailouts to maintain their dominance.

3. Decentralised Governance: Rather than relying on a coercive state to provide law and order, anarcho-capitalism envisions a world where governance is decentralised and voluntary. Communities would

organise themselves based on mutual consent, with private institutions providing services such as security, arbitration, and infrastructure. As discussed in previous chapters, there are historical precedents for such systems, and modern technology offers new ways to make decentralised governance even more efficient.

A Call to Action: Embrace Volunteerism

The state of the world today may seem bleak, but there is hope. By rejecting the coercive structures of the state and embracing volunteerism, individuals can begin to reclaim their sovereignty and build a freer, more prosperous future. This is not just a theoretical possibility—it is something that each of us can begin to do in our own lives. Here are some practical steps you can take to embrace anarcho-capitalist principles and contribute to building a stateless society:

1. Opt Out of State Systems: One of the most powerful ways to undermine the state is to opt out of its systems wherever possible. This could mean using decentralised currencies like Bitcoin instead of government-issued money, homeschooling your children instead of relying

on state-run education, or participating in peer-to-peer markets instead of state-regulated industries. Every time you choose a voluntary alternative over a state-run system, you are taking a step toward building a freer society.

2. Support Decentralised Technologies: Technological advancements are making it easier than ever to bypass state control. Cryptocurrencies, blockchain technology, and decentralised platforms offer alternatives to traditional banking, government surveillance, and centralised media. By supporting these technologies and using them in your daily life, you can help create a future where individuals are in control of their own data, finances, and communications.

3. Build and Participate in Voluntary Communities: Anarcho-capitalism is not about isolation; it is about voluntary cooperation. Start building or participating in communities that operate on the principles of mutual aid, private property, and voluntary exchange. Whether it's a local barter network, a private arbitration service, or a community-based security system, these initiatives demonstrate that we don't need the state to organise society. As these voluntary systems grow and spread,

they will provide a tangible alternative to the coercive structures of the state.

4. Educate and Advocate: The ideas of anarcho-capitalism are still misunderstood or unknown by many, but change begins with education. Share these principles with others, engage in discussions about the morality of state power, and advocate for voluntary alternatives. The more people understand the ethical and practical benefits of anarcho-capitalism, the more momentum the movement will gain.

Building a Stateless Future

The path to a stateless future will not be easy, but it is possible. It requires a shift in mindset, from one that

views the state as a necessary evil to one that recognises the potential for a world built on voluntary cooperation and free markets. By embracing anarcho-capitalism, we can move toward a society where individuals are truly free to pursue their own happiness, unencumbered by the coercive hand of the state.

The future of freedom lies in decentralisation, in rejecting the concentration of power in the hands of a few and empowering individuals to take control of their own lives. It is a vision of a world where justice is not determined by political elites but by private institutions that compete to provide the best services. It is a vision of a world where innovation thrives, where communities organise themselves based on mutual consent, and where the coercive power of the state is replaced by the voluntary cooperation of individuals working together for mutual benefit.

This is not a utopian dream—it is a practical reality that we can begin building today. By embracing the principles of anarcho-capitalism and rejecting the coercive structures of the state, we can reclaim our individual sovereignty and build a freer, more just society. The future is in our hands. It is up to us to choose freedom.